OLD IS WHAT YOU GET

Dialogues on Aging
by the Old and the Young

Also by Ann Zane Shanks

ABOUT GARBAGE AND STUFF

OLD IS WHAT YOU GET

Dialogues on Aging
by the Old and the Young

ANN ZANE SHANKS

Photographs by the Author

THE VIKING PRESS
New York

Other photographs from "A Portfolio of Photographs
of the Aged" by the author appear on pages ii, 5, 26, 29,
32, 35, 37, 40, 43, 46, 48, 51, 52, 55, 57, 60, 65, 68, 70,
71, 73, 74, 77, 78, 80, 85, 87, and 88.

FIRST EDITION

COPYRIGHT © 1976 BY ANN ZANE SHANKS
ALL RIGHTS RESERVED
FIRST PUBLISHED IN 1976 BY THE VIKING PRESS
625 MADISON AVENUE, NEW YORK, N.Y. 10022
PUBLISHED SIMULTANEOUSLY IN CANADA BY
THE MACMILLAN COMPANY OF CANADA LIMITED
PRINTED IN U.S.A.

1 2 3 4 5 80 79 78 77 76

LIBRARY OF CONGRESS CATALOGING IN PUBLICATION DATA
SHANKS, ANN ZANE   OLD IS WHAT YOU GET.
BIBLIOGRAPHY: P.   1. OLD AGE. 2. AGING.
3. AGED—UNITED STATES—INTERVIEWS. 4. AGED
—GREAT BRITAIN—INTERVIEWS. I. TITLE.
HQ1064.u5s514   301.43'5   76–963
ISBN 0–670–52268–6

To my husband Robert and my three children—
Jennifer, Anthony, and John.
May we grow old joyfully together
and with "gladness of heart"

ACKNOWLEDGMENTS

The author wishes to thank the people who so generously gave of their time for interviews. Without them, of course, this book could not have happened.

I also wish to thank the following organizations, individuals, and friends who went out of their way to cooperate and lead me to the right people and/or research material:
The Gray Panthers (Philadelphia, Pennsylvania); Ms. Susan Fallick (Dalton School); The Hudson Guild-Fulton Senior Center; the Jewish Home and Hospital for the Aged; Sondra Gorney, Director of the Information Center on the Mature Woman; Jack Ossofsky, Executive Director, National Council on the Aging; New York State Office for the Aging; New York City Office for the Aging; First Aid for the Aged, Inc.; Ralph Nader; Dr. Olga Knopf; Age Concern, London (Lewisham), England; Margo Astrachan; Joy Hornick; Ellen Galinsky; Rossmoor Leisure World, Laguna Hills, California; Lenox Hill Neighborhood Association, Project SCOPE; the East Harlem Council on Aging; Terry Morris; Rene and Albert Hague;
Marcy Olive, who cheerfully typed the manuscript; and Bob Shanks, who encouraged and advised in the line of connubial duty.

It's no secret of human behavior that most of us are unable to empathize truly; the gift of being able to put ourselves into the hearts and minds of others is elusive. How much easier it is to demand that others conform to the carbon-copy idea we have of ourselves; people should look like us, talk like us, think, feel, and—even—be the same age as we are—a safe social ghetto. This is where empathy fails and misunderstanding begins.

Thus, I am grateful to the people in this book who helped me to make the journey across the boundaries of generation and social position to discover the wonders in lives other than my own. Hopefully, you, too, may share some of my pleasure in getting to know them in *Old Is What You Get.*

Ann Zane Shanks

OCTOBER 1975
NEW YORK, NEW YORK

PREFACE

I have always dreaded the idea of growing old—a typical American attitude, I know. Old age in our country remains for most people what Simone de Beauvoir called "a kind of shameful secret." Until now aging has been a taboo subject, one that most of us avoid talking about or even thinking about. Uncomfortable as it feels, however, I must begin to accept that aging is to be expected. After all, if you live, old is what you get. Still, if it is difficult to accept old age in others, it is nearly impossible to think about ourselves as growing old. But it will happen. We are living longer. More than half of our population will be fifty years of age by the year 2000. The problems of today's fewer older citizens will be ours by the many millions in not too many tomorrows.

If we are a lot closer to understanding the physical process of aging—and so much closer that soon we will live decades longer than we do now—it is imperative that we begin to better the quality of those years. Will we live with emotional and economic security and productivity, in an atmosphere of acceptance and respect? Not if present conditions continue. Unless we begin to change attitudes dramatically, we know that we, too, will be mostly pushed aside, ignored, and unemployed.

To further my understanding of the aged (and, hopefully, to face my dread of the process), I went forth with tape recorder and camera, interviewed and photographed older men and women in various parts of the country and in England. I also interviewed children from eleven years to twenty-one years of age, choosing that group since by the year 2000 they will be moving toward their middle years and their peak powers in the society. I hope they will use these powers to improve the lives of their elders and eventually of themselves. And perhaps the old and the young have more in common than we acknowledge: often both live outside the mainstream of society.

To find my subjects, I traveled from the high-priced community of Leisure World in Laguna Hills, California, to bleak London housing projects; from the expensive apartment hotels rising high over Central Park in New York City to, finally, my last interview two flights up in a Manhattan tenement.

People, I discovered, were eager to talk, to let go—to give out memories—to share and enjoy. I met a few elderly people through social agencies dedicated to the aged poor, some of those people isolated and infirm. Others were known to my friends. I interviewed two of my children:

males, ages thirteen and sixteen, and also one parent of mine: male, age eighty-seven, Dr. Kushner. (All three were able to forget they knew me and talked freely.) An entire class of eleven- and twelve-year-olds participated. Questions about death and dying, fears, sex for older people, past loves, loneliness, and losses were among the subjects discussed with everybody.

I did not choose to interview celebrities. Fame and money have a way of cushioning the shock of declining activity and increasing isolation usually connected with growing old. Rare and gifted people such as Margaret Mead, Helen Hayes, and Charlie Chaplin are too exceptional to provide insights about the general problems of old people. The exceptions do bear dramatic witness, however, to the research findings of several doctors now studying the aging process: ". . . if a person is forced to retire (most have to, due to mandatory retirement laws), or if he feels useless, then his health, his interest in taking care of himself, and his urge to live may suffer. His decline may have nothing to do with age or genes."*

It is true that people who seem to weather old age well are the ones who planned ahead. Diet, exercise, and preventive medical care are additional significant factors. Keeping busy, maintaining contacts with friends and family are also vital to emotional health. Fortunately, not all old people *are* ill and poor; only 5 per cent of the plus-sixty-five population are forced to live in institutions.

Within the book's scope, it would have been

---

* Dr. Erdman Palmore, Duke University Center for the Study of Aging and Human Development.

impossible to interview members of every race, occupation, creed, background, income, and age group as in a sociological treatise. I have given only an indication as to the thoughts, problems, needs, and memories of only some of our older heroes and heroines, as well as those younger in years but not often lacking in understanding.

Members of the generation below twenty-one years old surprised me with their sympathy and awareness of the problems of the aged, though some were challenged to think about these sensitive areas for the first time.

The people interviewed exist and are real. So are their actual names. Interviews stand as recorded, edited only for clarity, brevity, and elimination of repetition.

The problem is: there are now more than twenty-one million Americans over the age of sixty-five. A third of these are over seventy-five —the age group that includes the majority of more than one million nursing-home patients. Seven million of these twenty-one million are impoverished or have yearly incomes of $3000 or below, which is the U.S. Department of Labor's definition of poverty. The average Social Security payments account for less than one-third of this figure.

Thus, one-third of our older Americans are living in despair, suffering physical, material, and spiritual poverty. Most of them were not poor until they became old. A few even refused public aid, smothering themselves in pride— others are unaware of their rights in programs that do exist.

What can we do about it? And does anybody care? The condition of nursing homes in this country seems to indicate that nobody does care

—very much. Supported mainly on public money, the 23,000 nursing homes are part of a booming private industry that grows on and on. A relatively young business, it had its beginning after the start of Social Security in 1935.*

After World War II the number of nursing homes grew, and this growth was further accelerated after Medicare and Medicaid passed into law in 1965. Medicare, financed through the Social Security system, pays primarily for hospital expenses associated with acute illness. In nursing homes Medicare pays for only one hundred days of post-hospital care. Many patients in nursing homes have had their payments cut off, due to cost saving by the Administration.

Medicaid (and people often confuse the two) is the big bonanza for nursing homes. Medicaid pays for long-term care, as well as hospital treatment for the poor. State rules for eligibility vary. In some states, particularly in the South, people are not able to receive Medicaid if they have financial assets. In major metropolitan areas nursing-home bills run from $600 to $1200 a month; even the wealthy would find it difficult to meet those costs. Payments from Medicaid go directly to the institution, not to the individuals, including a $30-a-month allowance for personal use that the patient never sees. The owners of the homes grab the money for laundry charges. Do you see the problem?

Nearly all studies and investigations have

revealed nursing-home care is less than high quality (which is about as polite a statement as one can manage). In many cases after state investigation, it has proved shockingly below standard. Consumer pressure has a substantial role in fighting to maintain constant inspection of nursing homes and to obtain money for alternative essential services, such as keeping old people in their homes within their communities. Losing one's home in one's home town can mean giving up one's freedom and self-esteem and forfeiting a last ounce of independence.

Home medical care is equal in importance to the need for homemaker services, offering help with such everyday demands as shopping, cooking, cleaning, and, perhaps what's most necessary, companionship. Medicare funds are not available for such programs nationally—though Washington, D.C., has one, as well as a few other cities. The need outstrips the availability. Congress is supposedly moving toward creating legislation to establish alternatives to institutional care.

Positive forces can shake and change governments. Ralph Nader, for one, has had fine success improving the safety of our cars and almost alone shook up our automobile industry. Lately he has turned to the problem of aging with equal fervor, producing a revealing report on nursing homes.

Unlike other segments of society, the elderly have never bothered to join hands and enforce their needs politically, ignoring their potential voter strength as 17 per cent of the population. Because of this a budget cut on any level of government—city, state, or national—usually means immediate reduction in any program for the elderly.

To protect themselves, the elderly must be educated. One steadfast group working in this direction is the Gray Panthers, with some 7000 members, old and young. Founded in 1970 to fight discrimination against the elderly, it is led by Maggie Kuhn, a sixty-nine-year-old Philadelphia ex-social worker. The Gray Panthers are dedicated to the belief that the old and the young have much to contribute to making society more just and humane. They also support the credo that older people are a great national resource, that "too long have they gone under-valued and unused." In 1973 they merged their activities with the Retired Professional Action Group, supported by Ralph Nader's Public Citizen, Inc. Currently you'll find them involved in many other programs, including experiments with life-styles (Maggie Kuhn, herself, is living with two women in their twenties), and Media Watch, which fights against television stereo-types showing old people helpless and decrepit.

Yes, something has to happen—ideally a positive change in our attitudes toward older citizens. To begin with, we need new laws providing national health insurance, including a complete overhaul of the vast deficiencies of Medicaid and Medicare. Consumers should be represented during future Congressional hearings when changes are proposed.

There are so many considerations needed for the neglected aging: better transportation facilities with special attention to lowering fares, making more convenient schedules, routes, and safety precautions. Interdepartmental communication among numerous governmental agencies dealing with the elderly must be improved and the activities consolidated; at present there are twenty-two different agencies in the Health, Education and Welfare Department in Washington, D.C., responsible for the aged. Emphasis on preventive medicine and rehabilitative care, with more psychiatric treatment, is required in our health programs. Jobs must also be provided for those who want to work and are capable of working—without loss of Social Security payments. These changes are only a fraction of what should be done.

In spite of the problems, I heard more optimism than self-pity in the voices of those I interviewed. Staff members of social agencies when approached for information were enthusiastic and generous. Professional statistics were replaced by sincerity, official charts by compassion in our discussions, a hopeful sign of change in the character of the new aging specialist. Perhaps the efforts of these new professionals, dedicated to human-kind, will result in an overall public change in attitude.

Life does come full circle. By refusing to see or care about those who are old, we deny our own chances for dignified places in society when we ourselves are old. Let us not forget the consequences; understanding, concern, and compassion should begin . . . now.

This book may be a tiny effort toward a beginning.

Ann Zane Shanks

CONTENTS

OLD IS
WHAT
YOU GET

INTERVIEW

DR. ROBERT N. BUTLER
Psychiatrist, Author, Gerontologist

THE PULITZER PRIZE FOR GENERAL NONFICTION WAS AWARDED IN 1976
TO DR. ROBERT N. BUTLER FOR HIS BOOK *Why Survive? Being Old in America*

Children throughout the world have a great many fears about aging. Some of them are built right into the folklore in terms of fairy tales: *Grimm's Fairy Tales*—the women characters particularly. Even so, evil is often incorporated in the masculine figures of mythological and literary presentations, never in terms of more honorable fiction. Relatively speaking, there are very few old heroes and heroines in classical world fiction.

Remember, the good fairy was young and beautiful. But witches are something else altogether. Sometimes witches come out in beautiful clothing, but they soon get stripped down to the evil they really are. There is a time when a child recognizes such a thing as death. But there is a distinction between fear of death and nothingness on one hand, and fear of aging on the other. Our culture has had a taste of both. And recently we've had almost a "facing death orgy," with lots of books and lots of TV programs and stories about how we have to face up to the right to die, or should cancer patients be told, and so forth. I think just around the corner there is going to be an "aging orgy," when we will be dealing with all the problems of aging—and all of them have to be dealt with.

Of all the age groups in this highly geographically mobile society, the elderly are the least mobile. Those who do move want to go to the so-called sun states: Florida, Georgia, New Mexico, Arizona, California, more recently Hawaii, and even some to Asia and Central America. But the median income for old people is about $2600 a year, which is about $50 a week. It's obvious that most of the studies of populations in Sun City, Leisure World, and the like, since usually they have incomes of $10,000 a year or more, show them to be a very special class. These expensive "ghettos" represent a very small percentage of the American population of old people, which numbers twenty million.

Some of the studies in these costly retreats show that the tenants are pleased to be there, reflecting the fact that it was their first choice. Moreover, it's quite clear from other studies, they wanted to purchase security from crime, and escape from noise and children. All in all, they wanted a calm old age.

From the larger social perspective, it's regrettable to have this kind of separation of age groups. I think it's just as unfortunate to have so many singles buildings, with saunas, swimming pools, and the like. Any device that fragments age groups adds to the fright about aging in the

United States. It is also destructive to the sense of continuity, to the sense of a life cycle, and the sense of the reality of aging. (People just can't stand birthdays.)

There's also a considerable amount of racism and a certain amount of anti-Semitism in some of these retirement communities, reflecting the attitudes of only a small group. But everyone certainly has the right to pick and choose freely from a range of housing arrangements.

After World War II many of the young marrieds pushed out of the cities into the suburbs, leaving older people behind in the cities. Many of these cities today are impoverished and plagued by crime. One out of twenty older persons in the United States lives under marginal and difficult circumstances. And 25 per cent of our health problems are in this over-sixty-five-year-old group, as well as 25 per cent of our suicides.

Another kind of ghettoization is on the farms, where there is still a lot of rural poverty among old people. Those who have been a little more successful may have moved into a small town and retired. Nowadays their land may be farmed by a tenant farmer and his son. Being old in a rural area is actually harder than in an urban environment. The health-care systems are not good, particularly in the Dakotas, New Hampshire, and Vermont.

In spite of the segregation of the elderly, it's a mistake of our popular literature to lament the end of the three-generation family, all living under one roof. That is a myth. In Colonial days there never was a three-generation family in the United States. The younger people who first came to these shores didn't bring their families. And they may have been everything from indentured servants to crooks. It is true that even today in certain cultures like the Amish and the Italians there is a tradition of families staying close together. There are other families that maintain contact (which we call the modified extended family), such as Jewish families, who phone one another at least once a week, with the majority of older people living about half an hour's distance from their children. But more and more we have nuclear families, meaning no connection with grandparents. It isn't realistic to talk about three-generation families unless there are living members. Consider: in 1970 a ten-year-old boy would have one out of nineteen chances to have four grandparents alive, but in 1920, the chances were one out of ninety. The average life expectancy in 1900 was forty-seven years of age. Today it's seventy-two years of age.

In a more agricultural and craft-oriented society, a grandparent was the only means of production, and one who controlled his own destiny. It was John F. Smith and Sons, Plumbers, or Shoemakers, or whatever. And it was Harry Farmer running his farm in Indiana with all his children working for him.

Nowadays we have a population of eighty million working for others. We don't have the same type of economic control over our destinies as we had in previous generations. Eighty million American workers have different bosses and employers. In no way are they related.

One idea that might help in understanding the problem of the aged is to consider them almost orphans, remembering that 25 per cent have no living relatives. (Seven per cent of the older people have never married.) When we say it's terrible that elders are dumped into nursing homes, we must realize that 50 to 60 per cent of such old people have no families. We can appreciate the difficulties of being both lonely and without protection in those situations.

Recent studies have told us that if you're married, you may have a better chance of survival in your old age. And that may not be because of the remarkable love that exists between husband and wife. They might fight like cats and dogs, but if Grandpa is sick in the middle of the night and needs a doctor, Grandma can call the doctor on the phone. It's much worse if there's no one to phone for him. He could be dead in the morning.

I invented a word—which I don't totally like, partly as others have used it—ageism. But it is a way of putting some public relations on the problems of both the negative attitudes that people have toward old age and the institutional prejudices: unemployment discrimination and bias in hiring, to name a few.

We have a massive cultural problem on our hands and one which all of us very soon will have to solve.

THE CAST

Old People

Lena Anderson, 75 years old

Hope Bagger, 84 years old

F. M. Bowers, 73 years old

Rosel Cohen, 68 years old

Roxie Cohen, 67 years old

John Howard, 69 years old

Juneth Johnson, 66 years old

Alice Keyes, 67 years old

George Keyes, 78 years old

Leopoldina Krause, 73 years old

Lillian Kromick, 86 years old

Dr. Louis Kushner, 87 years old

Mimi Martin, 88 years old

Susan Robinson, 88 years old

Arline G. Stephens, ? years old

Frederic H. Stephens, 96 years old

Fred Wooley, 68 years old

Young People

Janette Beck, 21 years old

Dayna Bowen, 15 years old

Kim Caughman, 15 years old

Willie Lazado, 15 years old

Lucy Merrill, 15 years old

Anthony Shanks, 16 years old

John Shanks, 14 years old

Dewey Thom, 12 years old

David Walker, 14 years old

Classroom, New York City private school:
11- and 12-year-olds.

Emily, Angela, Kathy,

Mark, David, Andre,

Aaron, Jan, Vivie, Alex,

Ilyse, Annie, Minard,

John, Laura, Andrea, and Marc

ABOUT THE CAST

Old People

LENA ANDERSON—75 years old.

She was a governess for a South American family with two children most of her working life. She never married. The one love of her life died young, and Lena never found anyone to replace him. She also lived in Europe with her employers. One year, when they returned to their country, Lena came to America, where she worked mostly as a cook-housekeeper.

A handsome woman, Lena now lives alone in a three-room apartment in a Harlem housing project: she continues to search for the good and the pure and doesn't understand the world today. She finds it harder and harder to find anything good—much less pure—anywhere at all.

HOPE BAGGER—84 years old.

She is a widow who lives alone in an interracial housing apartment standing tall over New York's Hudson River. She is the former New York chairperson of the Gray Panthers—a social and political action group of old and young, based in Philadelphia and dedicated to ending discrimination against the aged. Married twice and a former schoolteacher from Michigan, she lives in two tiny rooms, surrounded by hundreds of books and cardboard file boxes stuffed with carbons of letters to Congressmen, foundation directors, and friends. Hope is the mother of one son, now middle-aged, who is "much too old" for her. Her daughter-in-law is not too old. She is her best friend.

F . M . B O W E R S—73 years old.

Ms. Bowers lives in three rooms on the third
floor of a walk-up apartment in the suburbs of
London, England. The apartment windows face
a massive grassy green square. The decor of
blond Danish modern furniture, plants, and
books is most inviting. Ms. Bowers' intelligent
eyes, milky-white hair and skin contribute to her
attractiveness. She makes one think of a warm,
beloved school headmistress.

Lately she has become interested in Age
Concern, a new London political-action group
similar in purpose to the Gray Panthers in this
country, but so far functioning unknown to one
another.

ROSEL AND ROXIE COHEN—
68 and 67 years old.

They have been married about forty years. It's
a marriage that works well, though both admit
that theirs was no love-at-first-sight saga. Roxie
worked until recently in a school cafeteria, as did
her husband. He also used to drive a food
delivery truck to the same New York school.
Their apartment is in a public housing project in
Harlem. Wax flowers, calendars, and a TV set
dominate the crowded living room. Among
things they agree about is their granddaughter,
Dayna Bowen: she is "almost perfect."

JOHN HOWARD—69 years old.

John is an ex-railroad man whose bare, bleak single room one flight up looks out over a noisy and nervous street in downtown Manhattan. John is small. An accident has left him hunchbacked. He has a remarkably pleasant outlook, considering his meager existence. The Fulton Senior Center, with its Telephone Reassurance Program (volunteers make daily telephone calls to check on every old person listed) keeps John happy. Often he telephones the Center "just to cheer them up." He depends a good deal on those daily telephoned "Hellos" and "How are you's," and worries what he'd do if someone ever forgot to call.

JUNETH JOHNSON—

66 years old.

She feels that she has found her answer for a suitable life-style in the luxurious community of Leisure World in Laguna Hills, California. The community has manicured lawns, wide, empty thoroughfares, and guarded entranceways, making Juneth feel both aesthetically satisfied and secure. Security costs: one-bedroom houses are approximately $37,800 and up, to $58,400 for a three-bedroom house. Prices vary with architectural details and location. Ms. Johnson, a recent widow, is optimistic about her future. She is planning to revive her interest in the sports she enjoyed as a girl: tennis, swimming, and hiking. She might even do some politicking. There are unlimited possibilities at Leisure World.

ALICE AND GEORGE KEYES—
67 and 78 years old.

The Keyes are blissful about Mobile Park, which is next door to Leisure World and cheaper. Mr. Keyes, who once lived in Leisure World, felt it unfriendly and too expensive. "Your lawn is extra, and so is everything." He much prefers their present mobile home, which isn't mobile. It sits on an assigned plot of ground, with some grass, next to other trailers of different lengths, sizes, and colors—some with awnings and patios. Many of these dwellings look like metal frankfurters, and it's hard to believe they can be made to roll along highways. The floors of the Keyes vehicle are carpeted wall-to-wall, and their living room resembles an ad in a home-decorating magazine. A beloved daughter lives nearby, making Mobile Park that much cozier for the Keyes.

LEOPOLDINA KRAUSE—

73 years old.

She is a widow who worked hard most of her
life. These days there are no visitors except
fifteen-year-old Kim, who arrives once a week
from the East Harlem Neighborhood Council in
Manhattan. Kim runs errands for Leopoldina:
to the grocer, the laundry, and to the telephone
and Con Edison offices. (Kim earns $2.50 an
hour and works five afternoons a week doing
errands for other old people.) Ms. Krause
doesn't know what she'd do without her. Kim's
visits ward off total isolation, since all of
Leopoldina's friends are dead and no replace-
ments have come along. There's the radio. But
no television. Leopoldina is almost blind.

DR. LOUIS KUSHNER—
87 years old.

He was a dentist and has been married to my
mother for sixty years. My mother and father
still love each other, and I'm sure they believe
that marriage is a virtue and a strength. Though
sometimes turbulent, their marriage endures.
Nowadays they are desperately interdependent,
though my mother is more physically infirm
than my father. Her generation encouraged
women (for work was considered beneath them)
to entertain, to rest in bed and be waited on,
either by servants or by husbands. My mother
followed her calling. And she is still resting.

LILLIAN KROMICK—86 years old.

She, too, is widowed. With her husband gone
and her two children married and no longer
living with her, her life is barren. One can
appreciate the rich, warm voice rumbling along,
attesting to the success of her former singing
(and piano-teaching) days. Her days are spent
mostly alone. She enjoys recalling her past when
an occasional relative visits her.

MIMI MARTIN—88 years old.

Ms. Martin has been widowed for at least twenty years. Her courage is amazing: she escaped from the Nazis in the 1930s, came to America and supported herself, single-handedly, by working as a baker in a large hospital. Her son, now married and living in New York, is a gifted and successful Broadway composer. Mother and son keep in daily telephone touch. Once a week they play a fast game of bridge. Ms. Martin lives alone and is fiercely independent. She has something of the aristocrat in her speech and bearing. Her family treats her accordingly.

SUSAN ROBINSON—88 years old.

Ms. Robinson is a widow who lives on a middle floor in a high-rise luxury apartment hotel overlooking New York's Central Park, which once catered to the likes of Carol Channing and a collection of blond wigs; it now houses only older people accustomed to expensive living. Ms. Robinson's interests are still cultural: opera and music. Traffic and jostling crowds make it hard for her to attend concerts as she used to. When she ventures out alone, taxis pass her by. (Old people are thought to take more time and tip less.) Small and seemingly fragile, with coiffed pure-white hair, she remains the elegant lady. (That is a younger Ms. Robinson in the oil portrait above.)

MR. AND MRS. FREDERIC H.
STEPHENS—96 years old.

(Wife Arline did not wish to reveal her age.)

The couple live in a friendly apartment in Leisure World, Laguna Hills, California, where relaxing on their screened-in porch and gardening make life constantly pleasant. For most of his years Fred worked in the Philippines, heading his own import-export business. Because he did not heed a warning to return to the United States, he was captured and endured World War II in a Japanese prison camp. He wrote a book about his experiences, and General Douglas MacArthur contributed the foreword. Arline and Fred share most philosophies and the same diet. He is particularly hale and hearty at ninety-six years of age and believes in "moderation in all things."

FRED WOOLEY—68 years old.

He is a retired printer living in a one-room flat in a block of identical two-story brick houses, a half-hour outside of London, England. He's a bachelor who finds retirement ideal. He has time now to do things he loves—and at a leisurely pace: things like the daily watering of his plants and working the *London Times* crossword puzzle. These activities take up his entire morning. Before, not too long ago, he had had a difficult time getting over his mother's death. Fred had loved her deeply, and they had always lived together—until a few years ago.

THE CAST

Young People

JANETTE BECK—21 years old.

She is attending college. She hasn't made up her mind about what she is going to do in life. For a long time she was a responsible member of the Lenox Hill Neighborhood Association in New York, caring for old people on a paid basis. When approached for an interview, she wanted to talk about her grandparents, with whom she had chosen to live for most of her life. But she wanted to meet away from them, so she could speak more openly. She has spoken openly, indeed.

DAYNA BOWEN—15 years old.

Dayna is fortunate. Her family enjoys her free-wheeling enthusiasm immensely, and so do her many friends. She attends a private high school where she matches the accelerated and intellectual brightness of the other students.
Though she has conflicts with her family over dating members of another race, she seems the least likely one to develop psychosomatic colds or stomach trouble due to inhibitions. She loves life, and probably nothing will stand in her way of enjoying it.

KIM CAUGHMAN—15 years old.

Kim is shyer and more retiring than the other young people interviewed. She is a member of a large family; her father is a lawyer. She has dreams of being a lawyer, too, at least a legal secretary, but she is also dreaming about becoming a high-fashion model. So she is thoroughly confused about her future.

Kim works with old people on a paid basis after school. She seems to have a good deal of patience with her "clients." They all like her very much.

WILLIE LAZADO—15 years old.

Willie is Puerto Rican and lives in New York City. At first my questions about growing old baffled him, since he had "never thought about it." He had trouble articulating his feelings about aging, and recognizing if he had any feelings on the subject at all. Such matters were new to him. His younger sister had an equally difficult time, ultimately refusing to talk. Willie began to speak—finally—but he'd start being positive about an idea, then change his mind. He couldn't get over the fact that people discussed such things at all—especially at home.

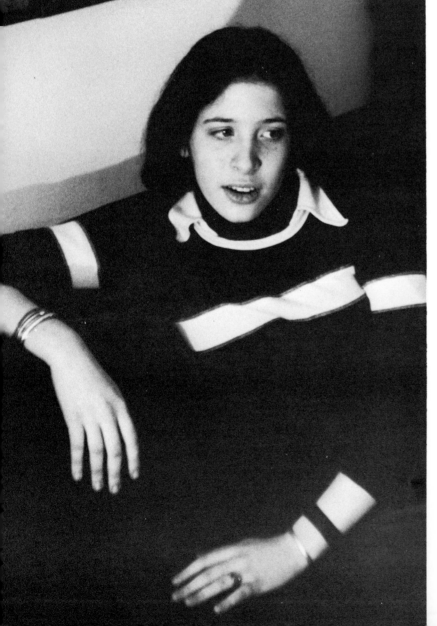

LUCY MERRILL—15 years old.

Lucy's the opposite of Willie Lazado. She is not only aware but exceptionally articulate. She is a student at one of the best East Side private girls' schools in New York and is familiar with the concepts of aging, death, and dying, in an intellectual way. But Lucy had personal experience as well. Her father died when she was five; she was brought up solely by her mother. An admirer of her mother's strength and intelligence (her mother is a professional writer), Lucy respects her heritage—particularly her one-hundred-year-old grandmother. Because of her better economic circumstances, Lucy is the only one working with old people without pay at the Lenox Hill Neighborhood Association. She finds it such a rewarding experience that she'd "pay for the privilege" of doing her job.

ANTHONY SHANKS—

16 years old.

I have known him all his life. He is one of my sons. Anthony is a redhead, an accomplished composer, and a fair pianist. Lately he has become interested in directing. This year he directed a scene at school from the Eugene O'Neill play *Long Day's Journey into Night*. He loved it. Anthony had not thought much about growing old before our discussion, but once involved, he threw himself into it with his customary élan. He was startled to discover he had not always been thinking too sympathetically about old people. It was a good time to start.

JOHN SHANKS—14 years old.

John, the youngest member of our family, is the one with a fine comedic sense. Formal school work doesn't excite him, but having a good time does. He is a good athlete and plays to win. His answers about aging were—naturally—on the humorous side, without his really meaning them to be. He is handsome and buoyant. John would like to be an actor or a radio disc jockey.

DEWEY THOM—12 years old.

Dewey is of Chinese heritage. I wanted to learn about his feelings about his grandmother (his grandfather is dead), but he explained there was a language and cultural barrier between himself as an American born here and his grandmother born in the old country. I found his inability to communicate with her true of many other Chinese-American children growing up in this country today. They just were not learning Chinese, or if they did, the dialects were too different to permit communication. In addition, many persons in the Chinese community appeared to resent their young's efforts to assimilate into the American culture.

Nevertheless, Dewey had an inborn sense and an acceptance of the life cycle: the idea of growing old and dying did not frighten him.

DAVID WALKER—14 years old.

David is a friend of John Shanks. He is quick, fun-loving, and bright. Through a nice friendship with an elderly doorman in the apartment house where he lives in New York, David has developed a positive feeling about older people. To him, older people are good for stories and surprises. His own grandparents have been doing "amazing things."

The articulate eleven- and twelve-year-olds I interviewed are enrolled in a private school in New York City, and I talked to them in their classroom. Almost all of these students loved talking about their grandparents, and they seemed also to enjoy them as people. Any complaints about the older generation centered on their grandparents' lack of understanding of their needs. As for the future: most of the students wanted to be lawyers, psychiatrists, economists, or scientists. Only one was interested in being an artist or an actor. After our interview the class was anxious to see the finished book. The students were even more anxious to know how to handle old people, both now and in time to come.

I'm not particularly interested in being old or whether other people are old or not. My life's concern has been for justice in society, and it just happened I got a job at seventy that showed me what old people are up against. Later I got into the Gray Panthers group through Maggie Kuhn, its founder, and wanted to continue the work she was doing. I like young people because they keep up with the changing world, and I, too, like to keep track of what's happening.

Two things are important when you're old: to have financial stability and to have good health. If you have too much pain, you can't do much. But I get angry when I think of those people who are perfectly well and competent who sit at Senior Citizen Centers and play Bingo. That gets me!

I've always been a defiant person. If I saw somebody in trouble, I tried to get after the person causing the situation and try to change it. I didn't take things lying down. I am an objector and always have been. I was the first married woman teacher in Detroit, Michigan. There was a rule that if you married and were a woman, you retired automatically. I didn't see any sense in that after I married, so I wrote to every member of the Board of Education and asked them what they were going to do about my marrying. I stayed.

You'd be surprised, but sometimes people are very kind to you when you're old. They do nice things for you. I've had two people at once on a bus get up and give me a seat. I can't occupy but one, although I look as though I could occupy two.

HOPE BAGGER, AGE 84

It's a world today that I don't understand. When there is no respect, there is nothing. There's too much freedom of everything: stealing, killing . . . everything. I feel sorry for the younger generation. Sometimes I get up and say, "I'm glad I'm old." I'm so much better off. There are so many nice, decent kids, both black and white, that don't get a break. I remember the days when you'd leave a club meeting at eleven-thirty, take a bus home at night, put your key in the door, and not a soul would bother you. Not today.

The Lord has given me so many beautiful people and moments; so if he takes me, I'm satisfied. I've lived to see a lot. The only thing I feel a little sad about is that I can't walk too well. But I'm very happy in my apartment. To me, I'm happy if I see the sunshine as it comes in here on my plants. They get so beautiful. It's always light in here in the day, especially in the summertime. I get all warm sitting at the window. I'm very content.

▽ LENA ANDERSON, AGE 75

I know people who are twenty-three and are like old bags. It's the attitude. As far as physically old, I guess I'd say anyone over forty is old. I consider my father old, and he's forty-eight. My mother's forty-one or forty-two, but I don't think she's old. Then there's an old man of seventy-four, and he'd get up and dance all night. That's more than I could do. You start getting old when you just give up everything. My grandmother doesn't even go shopping any more; my grandfather goes. And there's nothing wrong with her. She's making herself old, because she's losing all her outside interests. I don't know why. Then she complains about what my grandfather brings home from the store. And after she makes him do the shopping! "I can't climb the stairs," she says when I ask her why she doesn't shop with him. "Four flights." She's been drinking lately, too. Then she does everything backwards. She gets on my nerves.

I feel it's the children's job to take care of their parents when they're older. If you're married and a parent wants to come and live with you, it has to be decided between you, your husband, and your children. It's a big responsibility. I would never leave my grandparents or my parents completely alone.

I don't want my life to be like the old people I take care of through the Lenox Hill Neighborhood Association—Project SCOPE. Most of them have no one at all, or else they have children who don't care about them. I feel very sorry for them. So I want to have a big family when I get married, then I'll know there'll be people around me all the time. I don't want to be alone.

I'll probably be a grouch when I'm old. I think I'll be very moody, like I am now. I'll probably hang out of windows and throw things at people. I hope I'll have a family around to take my moods out on instead of some stranger. I'm very afraid to be alone.

JANETTE BECK, AGE 21

Now that I'm an older age, I'm reading much more and understanding much more. I can truthfully say that I am more aware of life today. I feel people more. There is a new humanitarian aspect in me, I'm beginning to feel sorry for people I was too busy to pay attention to before.

It's a terrible thing when you get older and realize you could have helped certain people, but were too busy, socially and professionally. My wife and I were pleasure-loving, and if there was anything worthwhile to see, we went. We neglected our children and missed an intimacy with them. We were too busy enjoying ourselves.

It would be better if I had played less golf in my life. I was an avid golfer, and I should have given it a lot less time. There was also a lot of social activity in my life which I would also give less time, leaving more hours for my family. I can't imagine I would've enjoyed it, but I should have tried.

DR. LOUIS KUSHNER, AGE 87

I don't know young people's ideas today at all. But I'd be interested to hear some of them.

LEOPOLDINA KRAUSE, AGE 73

I like anything that moves. I'd like either a plane or a car or a boat. That's my weakness. I'd like just to be able to get in one and go places. I'd like just to put beautiful people around my place. The people around me now, I think, are all beautiful.

JOHN HOWARD, AGE 69

I used to consider a person old at sixty. But here I am sixty-six and am still not considering myself old. I always wanted to be young and active. I have a lot of years ahead of me. I come from a long-lived family. My mother and father were both up in their eighties. I had a physical just before I moved down here. The doctor tells me I'm in perfect health.

When people get older, they are more or less forgotten. There are many older people who barely have enough to get along. I'm very glad I'm not in that position. They have no money for pleasure or recreation. Especially those who are ill. They're lying in hospitals—forgotten. Many of them even can't get into a hospital. And there's no one who looks after them.

I think our government could provide a better medical plan for the elderly so they can be taken care of and an illness doesn't take their last cent. I think things should be planned for them: recreational, cultural. There must be many who would love to participate.

I will probably get active in some political organizations like I did in my former town, hoping to help change and work for things to change. I am looking forward to being very happy. Let's say now I'm relaxed. I know now where I'm going. Doors are going to open up for me.

I'm happy there is a community like Leisure World for people as they get older. And I think that people who have raised families and had children, even grandchildren, a time comes, even though they love them, when they want to avoid being a burden on their families. In this community they can be independent and live their own lives.

The age requirement here at Leisure World is fifty-two, and there are a lot of people in their fifties. To me that's not old. I don't even consider myself old. As far as some of the real elderly people here, you don't see them much. They're not attending functions. The real elderly, and those not able to participate in activities, stay in their manors. So you're not looking at people and finding them old and depressing. I don't want to think about being old or about how long I'm going to live. I'm going to enjoy my life while I can.

JUNETH JOHNSON, AGE 66

I've never thought about being older than twenty. Of course, I've thought about getting married and things like that, but I never see myself living alone. I want to be around people even if I do get very old. I don't want to sit around in a house, even with somebody . . . just sitting around doing nothing. It's got to be in the city. Even if I become totally and completely disabled, I'd want to teach school, teach music, something. But I definitely cannot live alone. I don't ever want to become a castaway or not useful. I think no matter how old I get, there's never going to be a time when I can't make somebody smile. That's worth a whole lot to me.

I want to be fun for people to be around when I'm old. I want to work. I want to be the first something that nobody else is. I don't know what. I was the first girl on the swimming team. And I was the first one in the tenth grade to be on the Advisory Council. That makes me unique.

I would never pluck my eyebrows or lift my skin if I were old. But I wouldn't knock it if somebody else did. I'd be disappointed in my grandmother if she did because it would mean she didn't accept herself. I can't stand it if somebody sixty tries to act twenty. Or if somebody twenty tries to act sixty. I like it when people find beauty in their own ages, and inside themselves.

I've never met anyone who was scared of old people. I don't dislike old people for any reason. I don't like being preached to, if that has anything to do with it. I don't like being preached to about morals and ethics that are four years outdated. But I'll listen to anybody's point of view. I like listening. The Deacons' board at our church, for instance, is appalled at the length of our skirts, and our talking to boys after church. That makes me angry, when somebody places their own values on you. Or if somebody's not open-minded. I don't like not being respected just because I'm young.

DAYNA BOWEN, AGE 15

It's like, okay, there're three stages: when you're born, then you're a little baby, and then when you're about twenty, there's a decline. It's like being a baby, then a person, and then going back to being a baby again—like a baby can't walk and an old person can't walk either.

Everyone would like to be young and have fun. And be able to run. And when you're old, you can't run and you have to be careful what you do. And you go everyplace with a cane and with crutches or a wheelchair. You're a little scared, and there's nothing you can do. I'd like someone around in case of accidents.

JOHN SHANKS, AGE 14

I think honestly it's the attitude you bring to people. Two years ago I was knocked down by a young man who snatched my bag and off he went. All I could do was feel sorry for him. We have no big youth cult in Britain. There's a good deal of criticism of students in particular. Their long hair and how they get grants and do what they want with the money. I remember an incident one day when I was getting on a bus. The buses go by so quickly, I really feel a bit unsafe on them. While I was waiting for one, I was alarmed by a ferocious-looking young man behind me. He was eyeing me and I tried to inch away. Presently the bus came, the crowd surged forth, and didn't he put his great arms around me, pick me up, and put me safely on the bus despite my protests!

There are tremendous changes, and I'm prepared to accept them or at least wait and see what happens. One of the great changes is the freedom of speech and the allowing of young people to lead their own lives. There are, as a result, many one-parent households now. Another change is the breakup of family life. Still, I'm very happy when I see the old-fashioned family unit working well.

▽ F.M.BOWERS, AGE 73

It's hard for me to sympathize with old people, because I have not experienced what they have. I've never wanted to put myself in their place and feel what they might feel. I'm sure it's because growing older is closer to death. And I don't want to die.

Growing old is what I'm doing now, what I've been doing all my life. Expanding, experiencing, and continuing to grow the way I am. It's hard to imagine what I'll be like at thirty-five. I don't think one can, really. I feel sorry for old people.

Being old is not at all ugly. If it's ugly, I feel sorry that we feel that way. Then why should we live? Why don't we just kill ourselves at fifty?

At a party sometimes I think, "Who wants to talk to those old crones?" And other times I'm more open to things. When I was in Haiti I met an old woman. What a marvelous person she was, really excited about life, so I learned it really depends upon the person. I like a person with a sense of humor. When an old person comes into a room or party, it can be an experience, talking to them and learning what's happened to their lives.

I'd probably not want to live forever. I'd get bored.

ANTHONY SHANKS, AGE 16

I wouldn't want to be a burden to the younger generation. And I wouldn't want them to feel like they had to help me, though I'd want them to. I don't want to be dependent on anybody when I get old. Most young people forget about the elderly when they get old. They feel they just aren't useful any more.

KIM CAUGHMAN, AGE 15 ▷

Sometimes I can't remember the day we were married. People say, "That's old age." But it isn't. It's a lazy brain. Now you see, I could walk back to the Columbia Pictures studio and take a $32,000 camera all apart, and I could put it all together and run that camera. That was driven into my brain. It was a challenge. But if you ask me my name fast, I forget. I can't think back on most of the movies I worked on, because the titles were changed after they were made. I worked with some fine people: Humphrey Bogart, Lauren Bacall, Joan Crawford, Ernie Borgnine (he and I became very good friends).

GEORGE KEYES, AGE 78

If you have a good disposition and plenty of love, you won't grow old. You'll be taken care of. It all comes back to you. Do you remember Trixie Friganza? She used to make an after-curtain-call speech and say, "Just remember, cast your bread upon the water and éclairs will come back to you." This is our éclair—this apartment in Leisure City. If you live the right kind of life, you'll continue to be healthy.

ARLINE G. STEPHENS

I don't feel old, but my eyes, ears, and legs tell me I am. I had a big library, over one hundred books, but I can't read any more. My mind works all the time. When you get old, you lose your independence. But I'm lucky, my children and grandchildren are very nice to me.

MIMI MARTIN, AGE 88

I think children are having too much freedom. Parents today have become afraid of their children. They don't demand enough from them. They say, "If that's going to make him happy, let him do it." I don't think a child has common sense. When you're young, you think about getting somewhere, don't you? You should instill that in your children. If you tell your children that's fine, do anything you like, sometimes it works out; most of the time it doesn't. But I see so many people my age who have children and grandchildren. And to hear some of them, it's enough to break your heart. Thank God, I have been fortunate. But I'm one in a million.

I was finished bringing up the children, and I felt I could relax a bit. And I said to myself, "You are no longer a young woman and you can't be giddy or carry on. You have to be reserved. You're an old woman of fifty." Then one day I said, "What a dope I am, this is my time to live. I'm through with all my responsibilities. The children are grown and now I can go and do." And I did. I still wear everything the young people wear, within reason. I don't let myself feel old.

I think this women's lib business is a big mistake because I think most every girl who gets married eventually wants children. I think every child should have parents—both parents. I think even if things hadn't worked out and I had children, I would never consent to a divorce. I would rather suffer. I don't feel it's fair to the children. As a matter of fact when my daughter was divorced, I was more heartbroken for my granddaughter than I was for my daughter. At the time I wondered what kind of life she would have. And she has had a hard time of it, not having a father.

SUSAN ROBINSON, AGE 88

You finally see the light about old people when you reach forty. You see that you're going to be old in another thirty years and then you hope young people are going to be kind to you. My generation respected our grandparents; our parents made certain of that. I don't know if I loved them, but I feared them. They were the patriarchs. Today it usually is the grandparents who spoil the kids. If I were young again, I guess I'd like my grandmother to be more like my mother.

If you're single, you do feel rather frustrated that your life is a waste. You feel that what you've done has been to no end. Being single makes you rather selfish. You see yourself as the only person to look after. And if you have no children, you feel you have no loyalty to anybody but yourself.

The most important thing in life, as I look back on mine, is education, really, job education.

But what man really needs in life is just . . . self-respect.

FRED WOOLEY, AGE 68

I think most of us pass over old people too quickly. They just don't realize that there's anything there. They think that their lives are through, and they're not. They're old, and we're young, and that's it. We have a long way to go, while their lives are over. But they're not over. Until they die, life isn't over. If they're not dead, then they have to be dealt with.

LUCY MERRILL, AGE 15

I don't think it's any of the government's business to take care of the aged. I think it's the older people themselves who should have started taking care of themselves when they were younger. As long as people feel that the government is going to give them money, they won't take care of themselves.

FREDERIC H. STEPHENS, AGE 96

I'd like to set my death at four hundred years. When I'm four hundred, I'd like to look like I would at ninety today.

I believe in cosmetics for the old or face-lifts. I've told my father he can dye his hair if he wanted to make himself look a little younger. My mother can have a face-lift; it's OK with me. It depends on what they want. I'll respect them for doing it.

I say now that if I'm old and I have to be put

on a machine that's costing at least three hundred dollars a day to keep me alive, and it's ruining my family—then kill me. But I don't know whether I'll think that when I'm eighty years old and it happens.

Senior citizens' passes for free buses and movies are good ideas for old people. I treat them with respect when they're getting on or off a bus, but I also want to get them out of the way. I don't want to be bothered. I'd get old people more involved in community affairs, music, concerts, the arts, and theater.

I will feel what older people feel when I'm eighty. I have a lot of feelings, but I don't feel the physical things they do. Nor do I have the same experiences.

Knowing that I've lived eighty years, I'd want everyone to respect me. I'll probably feel that no one cares for me. I'll probably feel the same way that some old people feel today.

ANTHONY SHANKS, AGE 16

Things are different today. We didn't know about dope and drugs; all we knew was alcohol. Of course, we have more alcoholics in this country than we have addicts. Drugs and needles. We didn't know about things like that.

ROSEL COHEN, AGE 68

It's natural to grow old. You have to become old. You just can't stay young all your life. Growing old is just part of the life cycle.

I'd still like people to treat me the best way they know how. Young people should consider that when they'll be old they wouldn't want people to treat them badly.

◁ DEWEY THOM, AGE 12

I'm not going to let myself go to waste when I'm old. I'm going to try to keep in shape. There's a hundred-and-four-year-old man who used to jog around Candlestick Park beating the younger men. I'd like to do something like that. I have a chance to live a long life because my family on both sides lived a long time, usually to eighty or ninety. I'd like to live as long as I could, as long as I'm healthy. But mostly I'd like to be able to think and not have everyone doing things for me. It would be more fun to stay young, but you have to experience everything!

Being old means being unable to do as much as before, but it also means being more knowledgeable and understanding more. Yet, knowing life's not going to go on forever and there's nothing you can do about it, you try to put death out of your mind.

DAVID WALKER, AGE 14

Kids change with their age, just like we did when we were growing up. Now even the world has changed. Even in my day the only things we knew were the organ, the piano, and maybe we'd seen an airplane about once every two to three years. Then again, we had yards and fields to play in while kids today have to be cooped up. A lot's changed. Even we are changing.

ROXIE COHEN, AGE 67

MORE ATTITUDES

INTERVIEWS IN A CLASSROOM
Students Eleven and Twelve Years Old

KATHY:

I really don't think I feel that sad for old people because they have lived their lives and now they can relax and maybe do some of the things they always wanted to do. They've had a lot that we're going to have.

I wouldn't like my grandchildren going behind my back and saying, "Oh, she's getting senile. She's going crazy." I want to be treated just like they're treated.

DAVID:

I kind of feel a little detached from all the old people I know, and maybe a little scared of them. They're strange. They're different.

ALEX:

Old people are babied, they're not treated as equals. They're treated with "would you like my seat," and as if they can't do anything. Which is the opposite of what they'd like.

ANDRE:

When I grow old, I'd just like to be myself. I'd like to have a companion—like a wife or something.

ANDREA:

I look forward to getting old, but only up to a certain point—maybe to forty when you're a wife, have children, work, and have done a lot. But once I think about getting older, I get scared of how lonely I might feel. And how close I am to death. I'll wish I could start again.

I want to have a family around when I'm old.

ANGELA:

One of my grandmothers is very active. But when she was scrubbing the floor she hurt her knee. Now she has arthritis. If I were old, that's one thing I would really not want to get. With our joints, we can shake them around, but when you're old you can't move.

ANNIE:

When I think of growing old, I think of getting close to death.

ILYSE:

I wouldn't want everyone worrying about me when I grow old. I wouldn't want everyone calling up every night.

EMILY:

When I'm old I wouldn't want to be babied—if I wanted to get up and get a drink of water, I wouldn't want my granddaughter to say, "Oh, no, don't you do it—I'll do it."

If you really get sick, you might have to stay in bed all day, and then you might start feeling depressed. Then you might look out your window and see young people doing things. You might want to do them, too, but you can't. So it brings your spirits down. It doesn't help you get well.

AARON:

Most of us said that when we're old, we won't want somebody to get a drink of water for us. But when we do it for an old person, they don't mind. I don't know why we shouldn't.

I don't want to depend on anybody. I want to be myself. I don't want anybody to help me do what I want to do.

JOHN:

I'd like to be treated with courtesy. I wouldn't like to be treated like I'm old.

LAURA:

I wouldn't want to be treated like I'm in a separate category.

MARK:

Let's look at this realistically. Old people have got to accept that they're different. They're not as agile as they once were. So they can't be treated like they always were.

Who wants to live forever? Oh, my God, I'd hate it!

MINARD:

When I grow old, I'd like people to think that I can take care of their children, that I'm responsible.

VIVIE:

I don't want to be reminded that I'm old. I want to be treated like I'm about forty.

39

DEATH

My husband died suddenly of a terrible abscess. We had tickets for Italy on our twentieth wedding anniversary and he died the day we were supposed to leave. That was in 1931 and Hitler came in 1933. All the people I loved have died avoiding torture by Hitler. I left in 1941. It got so bad in Germany I had to leave or be killed because I was born a Jew. I got all my children out too.

MIMI MARTIN, AGE 88

When you're young, you deal with things more out of fear. My father's death hurt me so much and so did missing him. I remember the funeral. I told my mother about the coffin: that he didn't have enough room to move around. You don't think about things like that when you're older. My mother spent a lot of time telling me that nothing about his death mattered, because he no longer felt pain. So I just got used to the idea as a sort of finale. It was something that should happen, eventually, with everyone.

My mother just cared a lot. She was there—she's very strong. And she was there enough, so that I became very strong. Now I feel that death is no longer scary. My mother's done about the best job anybody could in replacing him. She's about *three* people. And she's always been there when I needed her, even when she was working. It's not like I was the only person who's ever had a death in his family. You have to get over things and you have to move on. I guess you can't sit around and feel sorry for yourself all the time. We certainly have an easier time of it than . . . half the world.

LUCY MERRILL, AGE 15

I'm not afraid to die. I'll have nothing to say when my time is up. Even if I would be afraid, it's going to come. And I'll be there. We all have to die, even the King and the President and all of them are going to die. Are we any different? It really doesn't worry me.

LEOPOLDINA KRAUSE, AGE 73

My husband had cancer. He knew it. Nobody told him. He never asked me because he didn't want me to feel bad. But he told the neighbors. He said, "I know what's wrong with me. It's taking too long now." After he died I found five birthday cards and five aniversary cards he had left in my drawer. And an Easter card for the next year and Christmas card that said, "You remember what Christmases we used to have?" And still another card said, "Speedy recovery." The speedy recovery was on top of all the cards.

LEOPOLDINA KRAUSE, AGE 73

About five months ago my grandfather died. I mean I think of it. You're sad, you're crying. It's unbearable, you want to kill yourself. It was nothing for him. He lived. He died. That's it.

If there was a nuclear war, I'd shoot myself. If it's my decision to do so, then I wouldn't be afraid. But I'd really like to die in my sleep.

Classroom interview
(tape recording unclear, name unknown)

I don't want to survive my children. I have lived from 1887 till now. And when I was a child, we had kerosene lamps, but we didn't have electric lights, no telephone, radio, or television. I've lived through some rapidly changing times. I have no idea what is coming. Really, I'm sorry that I have to die soon, very soon.

MIMI MARTIN, AGE 88

My life with my husband was a very good life; I understood him immediately. He was a chess player, and chess meant more to him than anything in the world. He loved his children; he loved me, but if he had to play chess, he forgot he had a home; he forgot he had children. And I understood. A month before he died, he put his arms around my waist and said, "From now on, darling, not too much chess. From now on I'll be your eyes." But one day, a month later, he died. So I had no one to help me. Two months later my daughter married and moved away. That was the one thing I was sad about and resented. My son married five years later. By now I should be accustomed to being alone.

LILLIAN KROMICK, AGE 86

I'm a little scared. I don't want to die. If I do, I want to die peacefully in my sleep. No heart attack or something. You know, go *Ahhhhhhhchk* and then you're gone. If I have to go, the funeral's going to be OK.

You wish there was life after death so you can leave this planet and go to the next. (Maybe you start off as a butterfly and then a "horsy.") But how can you go to another planet if you dry up in your grave and all that's left is bones?

JOHN SHANKS, AGE 14

I think it's terrible that people are always mixing up dying with sleeping. When I was little, I'd get upset and say, "Oh, I'm gonna die. Something else to add to my problems." I'd hate it when they'd say they put their dog to sleep. When I was six, I remember sitting on my bed and throwing my head into my pillow, and crying, "Oh, I'm gonna die!"

I'm not scared of dying now because I don't know what it is, so how could I be scared? I'm not for it, but I'm not against it. It's an experiment. You might get reincarnated. Who knows?

MARK
Classroom interview

I'm afraid of dying because I don't know what happens after death. That's what I worry about. I know I don't want to be buried. I want to be cremated. I have this fear of bugs. I just can see bugs crawling on me in the ground. You see I don't really know that if I'm dead I won't feel them.

JANETTE BECK, AGE 21

Nobody wants to die, but you're gonna die someday. You just have to be thankful, you know, for the days you live.

ROXIE COHEN, AGE 67

When you lose consciousness, there is nothing. You know there is nothing. You have no action and you seem to wake up out of nothing. My husband always said dying is not difficult. His last words were, "I feel wonderful." I know death must come soon for me, but it's no pleasure.

MIMI MARTIN, AGE 88

When I think about dying and what it's going to feel like, I realize it may not feel like anything at all. I can't picture that. I have nightmares about it.

I just can't imagine doing nothing. My mother and father said that it must be like being in a deep sleep, except you can't dream. It's scary.

Classroom interview
(tape recording unclear, name unknown)

I'm not afraid to die. If I were to die this second, I would say, "Thank God, I'm through with it." The only reason why I'm afraid to die is wondering who is going to take care of my wife. She is very dependent on me. Cruelty in old age is being left alone.

DR. LOUIS KUSHNER, AGE 87

I wish nobody would ever die, but there's a time you have to pass away. But I don't want to die, really. I wouldn't want God to take me now—I'm too young. But I don't think I'll ever want to go at any age, because I'm scared of the thought of being dead and the casket and being put into the ground. I don't know if I'd want to be cremated. But if I did, I'd want my ashes given to my children.

KIM CAUGHMAN, AGE 15

It's not that I'm afraid for myself, but I have set great goals for myself. I have social plans to save the world from starvation. I've been alive in this world, an active individual, relatively, for twelve years. I think it would be ingracious for me to die. And besides, I don't want to die anyway.

ALEX
Classroom interview

We know not a living soul on this earth who wants to leave this heaven and hell. But as sure as you're born, you've got to leave here. It doesn't bother me. The only thing I worry about is that I hope God doesn't keep me here to suffer. Maybe He would take me away in my sleep. My mother when she died didn't suffer and she lived to be eighty-three years old. She went like [snaps fingers] that.

ROSEL COHEN, AGE 68

Maybe if a lot of people would think about dying, they wouldn't be so mean and cruel. When you're mean and hateful, your conscience isn't clear so I guess it worries you.

▽   ROXIE COHEN, AGE 67

My father used to say: "Son, nothing on earth will take you away quicker than 'worration.'" (Worrying.)

ROSEL COHEN, AGE 68

Sometimes I picture myself in a car crash and I try to imagine myself dying, and it's so hard.

EMILY
Classroom interview

I don't want, at least I hope I never have to—to wait to go, so that I waste away till I'm a mere skeleton. That's what happened to my mother. I mean that wasn't my mum who died; a skeleton died. My mother was big and smart. At ninety-one she was finally taken away to a nursing home. Before that, there was only myself to look after her. She was almost helpless. But she still managed to break a window with her stick as the van took her to the nursing home. She lived four years longer, hating every minute. She wouldn't die, you know, just from sheer cussedness. We really liked her, my two brothers and I. She was never behind in anything that was new. We were the first family for miles around to have a crystal radio back in 1922.

FRED WOOLEY, AGE 68

I've thought about dying sometimes. I know there are two places we go: heaven and hell. I don't want to go to hell. To get in heaven, you have to be good. That's what I heard. You gotta help people, be kind. When they need money, hand it up. In heaven there are clouds; you can sleep all the time if you want to; you don't have to do any chores. When I die, I hope I just go to sleep and not wake up.

WILLIE LAZADO, AGE 15

I think you're reconciled that it has to be. You don't like it. I'm scared to death of it. I often wonder how it will happen to me. Will it happen during the day or the night when I'm alone? Will I be very sick or will I have to be hospitalized? There is fear. Everybody who tells you they're not afraid is not telling you the truth. From the day we were born we were brought up with, "If you don't behave yourself, God is going to punish you." I still remember those words. And if you're good and behave yourself, God will not only love you, but do things for you. Then you'll go to heaven. That's what my grandma told me as she washed and combed my hair. She also added that I would meet a good man and get married and have children of my own. "If you're a good girl."

SUSAN ROBINSON, AGE 88

Youth is tremendous, experiencing everything. Now, because I am young, I'd like to experience more, so then I'll have other experiences to look back on. I don't want to die at all.

◁   ANTHONY SHANKS, AGE 16

I'm not afraid to die. I think about it every day. And I talk to my children about it. Once in a while I think I'd like to wait to see my granddaughter Lisa get married! But Lisa might not get married at all. Today they don't worry about marriage. The only thing I'm grateful for is that I still have my mind.

LILLIAN KROMICK, AGE 86

Nonexistence frightens me most. Not being able to do the things I do or did. Not being able to have any sort of personality. Not being able to come back after I die. (Unless there are such things as psychic phenomena or ghosts.)

DAVID WALKER, AGE 14

I don't like to say that Mr. Johnson, my husband, died or that he's dead, so I say he passed on. His body may be dead, but his spirit is not. As far as I'm concerned, he has gone on to another world. To me, he is not dead. I will meet him. I don't know if he'll recognize me, but that is my interpretation. Sometimes I think about dying, but I'm not afraid. I don't know if you would call me a fatalist, because I feel our time has been planned for us before we were born. And when my day comes, I could be in a boat or an airplane or whatever; when my time comes that will be it. I hope that I can leave peacefully. I hope I don't suffer.

JUNETH JOHNSON, AGE 66

FEARS

I'm afraid to die because I have been brought up in a home where there was no God and the only life we have is the present. So it's hard for me to imagine death. I'm *very scared of it*. Because I don't know it and I haven't experienced it. There is no life after death. So my philosophy now is to live life to the fullest. If I had another life, then I might not live this one to the fullest.

ANTHONY SHANKS, AGE 16

I always lived with people; first my mother until I was twenty-five, then my wife, and then others. I have no regrets not having children. They might go away or they might die. Being older doesn't bother me. I have no regrets. I'm just scared of not knowing whether I'm going to have a friend tomorrow or not. My neighbor checks me every day. But suppose he disappears some night or moves out? What would I do? Everybody is too far away to come and check on me. I don't hear from the people at the Senior Center on weekends, and that's the time when most people get sick. I saw it happen in this building. Someone died one weekend alone, and no one knew it. I'd have liked someone to be around if that were me.

JOHN HOWARD, AGE 69 ▷

I'm afraid of feeling useless when I'm old. Not just in the future, but now. I'd hate to feel like I had no purpose, that I wasn't needed by somebody for something. I need people and I would like them to need me.

DAYNA BOWEN, AGE 15

When I think of being old, I'm afraid of not having control of my faculties, such as eyesight, hearing, and physical steps, more than physical steps, the use of my arms and my legs.

ALEX
Classroom interview

FRIENDS

After my husband died, I felt terribly lonely. It's a very big responsibility to turn everything upside down. We used to have a lot of friends where we lived. You know why? We entertained a lot. And when you entertain, you always have friends. But when you don't, you have none. And when people know you need them, they don't care. Now I really need them. I had quite a few nice friends, and they died away.

The new ones in New York where I moved to—that's like catching a fly: here today, gone tomorrow. I used to go to the Lighthouse for the Blind before I broke my hip. (I have two cataracts and don't see well.) I got hit by a truck. There are people at the Lighthouse who are not any better.

LEOPOLDINA KRAUSE, AGE 73

GRANDPARENTS

My Grandpa Jesse is not as healthy as he was, but he's mentally active. Maybe even more so, because now he doesn't have to have a specific occupation. He's in one of those old-people villages called Century Village (I call it Cemetery Village). . . . A lot of the people there are totally shut off from the entire world.

ALEX
Classroom interview

When my grandmother and grandfather come to our house, we're restricted from doing things we really want to do, because they're so scared. Except for my grandfather, he's active except he can't take commotion; then he starts raising his voice. We have a ninety-six-year-old neighbor in the country who's always wanting to come to our pool and swim.

ILYSE
Classroom interview

Whenever I see an old person, I feel sad for them. They have to stay home so much because their bodies aren't strong, so they can't do everything they did when they were little.

MINARD
Classroom interview

I feel sorry for them too, because if my grandmother, who's in her eighties, gets a fever, I think she could die. They don't have as good a chance as we do to recover.

ANNIE
Classroom interview

We really do love my grandfather; I'm not kidding you. Oh, my mother and grandfather and I are constantly arguing about something. I think we couldn't survive if we didn't argue. That's the fun of it. We argue about trivial things, like, "You broke a dish," or things like that. He thinks I'm a lost cause. And I think he's a foolish old gentleman. I usually say, "I'm sorry, I was only teasing," or something like that. I guess he loves me, because even if I'm the "wrongest" person in the family, he'll be on my side.

DAYNA BOWEN, AGE 15

They're a little kooky. Well, their brains, you know. They're getting older and they can't function as well. Some of them turn to drinking and really don't know what to do.

JOHN SHANKS, AGE 14

49

Since my parents lived with my grandparents when they first married and my mother worked, I got used to living with them. I never wanted to go home and still haven't. My grandparents are both about seventy-one, but my grandmother is an old seventy-one. She doesn't understand what people are doing today. She thinks I shouldn't be going to college but be married and raising children. My grandfather is a younger seventy-one, and he thinks what I'm doing is fine. I still like living with them better than with my parents, but as soon as I get enough money together, I'm going to get my own apartment. I have no privacy. And their opinions about things are so different from mine, so I no longer talk about my problems. But I still call my grandmother "Mom."

JANETTE BECK, AGE 21

Mine are making a lot out of their lives which I think is good for them. Take my grandmother. Her husband just died recently. And she has two boyfriends already. And my other grandfather is in California. He's, I think, about seventy. He just got married again. He got divorced and got married again. That's pretty good to be that old and feel you're so young at heart.

DAVID WALKER, AGE 14

I have this grandfather and grandmother, and they're not exactly old, but they're clutching onto their lives so dearly. I broke my pinkie and they thought it was the end of the world. And it didn't hurt! They must be afraid to lose me.

AARON
Classroom interview

I don't think old and young people understand each other. My grandmother says, "Well, when I was little, I had seven hours of school a day and I did this and that." She always wants me to do what she did when she was young.

Classroom interview
(tape recording unclear, name unknown)

They seem to think that just because they're old, they can demand respect. You know, "Respect your elders." Everybody should respect everybody. This is one of my constant fights with my grandparents. They say, "You have no respect for us. . . ." I say, "You have none for me." How can you respect someone older if he doesn't respect your rights?

JANETTE BECK, AGE 21

My grandfather is in his late eighties. He's pretty deaf. Whenever I go over to visit him, he always tries to act cheery. He used to be a mathematician. I always like to watch him make drawings. He likes to show me how to draw. We're really pretty close. I feel sorry for him because he doesn't go out any more. He just spends his time resting, or sitting.

Classroom interview
(tape recording unclear, name unknown)

My grandfather, I like him a lot. When I break something (he lives with us) he helps me fix it; he doesn't treat me like I'm really little—he tells me how he fixed it, and wants me to fix it myself.

MINARD
Classroom interview

The individual is the main thing. Maybe we should stop counting or something. I'm so much like my grandfather. But my grandmother and I are more alike than anyone. But because she's got sixty-six on her Social Security and I've got fifteen on mine, we've got to be different. My grandmother will come to our house and we'll gang up against my mother. I love laughing with her. I tell her the same kind of jokes that I tell my best girlfriend. And I love to talk about boys with her. She likes to hide her sex life, and I hide mine, too, but we get together and tell secrets just like she was fifteen or I was sixty-six. And one thing she's learned not to do is say, "I can't tell you—you're too young." There are differences, yes. But that's because we're two different human beings.

DAYNA BOWEN, AGE 15

GROWING OLD

My father died when I was five. So I'm familiar with death. It's not like I've looked forward to it. It just hasn't seemed scary. I don't think I could stand *not* getting old. I don't think I could stand looking in the mirror after years and seeing my face being just like this. It just seems such a natural process to me; it would scare me more if I didn't.

LUCY MERRILL, AGE 15

Life has passed me by so fast that I didn't realize I was getting old. Age meant nothing to me. I live each day to the fullest. I don't feel old most days. I still play golf. I can still go out, only not as good as I used to. I don't have to have anybody help me across the street yet. I don't have to have anybody tell me what I should do. I still drive my car to Florida every year, but time forces you to change. You can't do the things you want to do, and it does bother you. The bad part of life is that my wife is not well and can't do the things I can do. She can't walk more than two blocks at a time, and even then I have to hold her up.

DR. LOUIS KUSHNER, AGE 87 ▷

Growing old is difficult. It's like walking to a river's edge; you can walk right into the water and no one will know what happened to you.

▽ SUSAN ROBINSON, AGE 88

HEALTH

The blind can't see; they imagine they see. I could see to go to the market until a month ago. I manage alone, but I suffer. I even keep house; it's very clean, I think. But I feel what I do. Now my elevator man takes me to the store. I was wearing a white nightgown; all the time I was wearing it I thought it was pink. We think we know what pink is or what red is; we imagine our own idea of the color.

LILLIAN KROMICK, AGE 86

My eyes have been a source of trouble over the past ten years. I was operated on and now the doctor is afraid to take a chance; I've got hemorrhages in back of one eye. It's natural. You don't grow old being well all the time. You have sick days and there are many days when you think, "Well, maybe this is the day."

SUSAN ROBINSON, AGE 88

I usually do feel well and my eyes don't bother me so often. The only thing that bothers me is that I can't read in bed because I have to take my glasses off and nowadays I need two magnifying glasses in order to read. I can't see your face at all. I take things as they come. Every age has its advantages. People at eighty-three are just about the same people as they were when they were forty-three or twenty-three or whatever. So you have advantages at every season. I used to be ill more of the time than I am nowadays. I used to get bronchitis because I didn't give in to a cold. I used to get a lot of headaches, too, but not any more.

HOPE BAGGER, AGE 84

It would be better if I had a few people to understand me and I could enjoy some friendships. Maybe we could visit one another's homes and even tell little jokes. We could even have a little lunch or coffee sometimes. I would also like to be healthier: I can't see; I have a hip injury and arthritis. Yes, the old are aching.

And for me, everything is in the dark . . . most of the time.

◁ LEOPOLDINA KRAUSE, AGE 73

HUSBANDS

In my day being in love didn't matter much. I never thought of it. A girl got married for security. My husband-to-be was a very good man with a very good reputation. At that time he was in the real-estate business. Later, five or six years after my daughter was born, he decided to go into the oil business. I couldn't believe it when he woke me up one morning at one o'clock after playing cards with a nephew and said, "I'm going to Oklahoma to go into the oil business." And so he did. The next day at 5:00 A.M. he left. I tried to discourage him, but he was hard to discourage, though he did become very successful. While he was gone, I collected rents from the property he owned just as he had taught me the morning he left.

He was kind and good to me. There wasn't a thing in the world that he wouldn't have given me. He gave me assurance and he gave me such love. The day before he passed away, he was sitting on the couch watching television, and he said, "You know, Susie, I'm tired and I think I'll go to bed now." He picked himself up to walk into the bedroom; he took me by the hand and walked over to my portrait and said, "You know, you're still a pretty good-looking girl. And I love you the way I loved you from the day I met you." Now, that's something you don't find very often. He was that way. And I miss him very much. I miss him a lot. There's not a minute in my life that I don't feel he's right at my side telling me what to do when I'm in a quandary. It's hard to understand, but that's the truth.

I used to call my husband the rubber ball. He'd bounce up and down, up and down. He was brilliant. He tried everything in the world. Nothing was too difficult for him. He once successfully drilled for oil and fifty-nine gushing wells came in; then he woke up one morning to discover that fifty-nine wells were dry. Many of the investors committed suicide. It was a terrible time. He called from Oklahoma and told me to prepare for trouble. "I'm afraid we're going to have a hard time," he said. I said, "Don't worry about it, just come home and we'll be all right." So he came home. One day we were walking down Broadway near Wall Street when we met an old friend of his. He said, "Robby, what are you doing with yourself? I heard you became a millionaire. I have an office on Wall Street. Any time you want to come in with me, you're more than welcome." He went in with him: H. T. Baker and A. Robinson. Together they made some of the largest real-estate deals this city ever had. I tell you, he was like a rubber ball.

SUSAN ROBINSON, AGE 88

He was the most marvelous man. He was good to me. He would just shower things on me, and he was so thoughtful. It would be hard to find another like him. I had a very happy thirty-three years. He was a highly respected man, a member of several organizations, a born leader.

JUNETH JOHNSON, AGE 66

My husband died in the hospital. I had held him in my arms and told him, "I'll come tomorrow morning. I'll come at lunchtime. I'll stop working at eleven and come." I told him that I'll bring him some orange juice, fresh orange juice. I'll make it myself. I'll bring it in a thermos bottle.

"Because," I said, "you want to get well and get your strength back. And you want to get home." He said, "Yes, I want to go home." It was 8:25 P.M. when I left the hospital that night. I walked about three blocks and I took a bus in the other direction to my home so nobody would see me. I didn't want the neighbors asking me how he was coming along. My husband had told them he would be home in two weeks. At 11:00 P.M. the telephone rang. It was the hospital. He was dead. I remember when I held him in my arms, thinking I heard rattling and assuming he still had a cold.

LEOPOLDINA KRAUSE, AGE 73

LIFE-STYLE

I'd like to live in a house in the country and be physically in good shape. I'd like my wife to be with me and a maid who comes in to help me. Help us. And a car. I'll probably watch football, or go for a walk or a drive. Or play golf. Maybe a little tennis or badminton or croquet. Listen, you can't do much when you're eighty.

JOHN SHANKS, AGE 14

When you get older, what do you talk about? You talk about your children . . . or your operations and what you've been through in your life. Most have nothing else to talk about. For instance, if I meet somebody who's musical, I can sit for hours and talk about music and forget all my troubles.

I can look back to when I was a young girl. My parents were poor. My father left Russia when he married. But they wanted to take him into the Russian Army, so Grandma stole him out of the house and they got him across the border to Germany. Lots of boys did that in those days. So you see, I came from very humble beginnings. I can remember where we lived. We had a little lamp filled with kerosene.

I don't say I wouldn't want to live ten years longer. Maybe I would. Many things are in the making. You see your children and grandchildren growing up. There's a great desire to see what's going to become of all this. It's something like the work of a lifetime. You do look forward to it. I can go and see my two wonderful little grandchildren. And I get such pleasure out of it. I go to bed and say, "If God will only keep me old enough so I can see what's going to become of them." And you do, you have a great desire. The happiest thing in my life right now is being with my children and grandchildren.

SUSAN ROBINSON, AGE 88

When you work all week like my husband and I did, we had no desire to go out in the evening. When I came home, I prepared supper, and my husband helped me dry the dishes afterwards. Maybe there was something to mend. He went in the den and listened to a program, and when it was ten o'clock, we might have a cup of tea and a piece of cake, and then we went to bed. In the morning we had to get up at a quarter to six because we went to work. Now what else would you do? You can't bum around at night and go out when you have to work.

LEOPOLDINA KRAUSE, AGE 73

However my parents want to live when they're old, I'll accept. Because it's their life. It's not mine. I think they'll probably be living outside of New York—Italy, Switzerland, maybe. Hopefully, my father will be writing still and my mother doing what she wants to do: directing, producing, photography. If they can. If they can't, they could sit around and read all day, using their minds. That's what I want most for them, to be able to use their minds.

I imagine I will be working when I'm old, or living in a big house or in some room where old people would be respected. I don't think they are today. If I could use my hands and my legs, I'd work. I'd get involved in society; and hopefully not be considered old, or waste my mind. When you're sixty or seventy years old, you have set values—your own ideas and opinions. Some people are very stubborn at that age. But others are open to new ideas. I would have more wisdom and knowledge by seventy years; that's to the good.

ANTHONY SHANKS, AGE 16

You have to admit when you grow older that you also grow better. Better, because you have time to ponder and forget your sins of omission. They are in the past. I don't scold my wife as much as I used to, and she doesn't scold me as much as she used to. She'd scold me because I didn't take my nap. I admit she did it because she loved me and wanted me to take care of myself. And I'd scold her because she did too much work. I'd do it probably for the same reason. In this day and age Arline and I get along very nicely.

FREDERIC H. STEPHENS, AGE 96
▷

The Telephone Reassurance Program at the Fulton Senior Center is one of the best things because it helps everybody. You can also go to the Senior Center in the morning and have breakfast. Or you can have lunch. You have a place to hang out, and you can play cards, too. They take care of you when you're sick. Sometimes they take you for trips and it doesn't cost too much. What's good about the Center is that they check in to see if you're all right. It's nice to hear somebody rapping on the door to say, "How are you?" or "Good morning"—a nice feeling.

Sometimes I read and sometimes I write or fix up my stamps, or I talk to somebody on the phone or somebody comes to play cards. Or they just stop and talk. I'm content. I've got nothing to lose.

JOHN HOWARD, AGE 69

When I first arrived in America, I was a cook-housekeeper. Then I worked in Mount Sinai Hospital as a baker. I earned $85 a month, and sometimes I sent my son Albert some money. He had nothing and was living in Cincinnati with my sister-in-law, studying to be a composer. At night I went to dietician school and became a dietician until I retired nineteen years ago.

MIMI MARTIN, AGE 88

What bothers me as you grow older is that inability to get about like you used to. You can't afford a car—at least I can't. Then you are bound to the bus, and it takes a wait of twenty minutes to half an hour for it to arrive. The journey may take only ten minutes. So shopping becomes a bore.

Organizations like Age Concern in London are putting telephones into old people's homes and paying the bills. But many of the elderly aren't able to operate the phones or dial 999 for help. Look, if I'm lying on the floor unconscious, I can't bloody well dial, and if I'm dead, I'm not interested.

When some of our club members were younger, they were heads of families. They had to work, do things for themselves. It's that stopping of doing things for themselves that makes them grow old and dependent. There's a club that I go to outside London on Wednesdays. There are about thirty people there over sixty-five, sitting around on their own chairs. If you sit on a chair, somebody comes along and says, "That's my chair." That shouldn't be. You should have a feeling that you're going there for pleasure, not to fight over a chair. Then lunch comes. It costs less than twenty cents a portion. As soon as the food comes in that door, they all dash as though they've never eaten a meal in their lives. The two blind men are left in their chairs, while the others eat at the table. That isn't what a club is for.

FRED WOOLEY, AGE 68

I'd like to live in the country. I like the excitement of the city, what it offers. The country is really not so quiet and peaceful. It's just more me. This is something my mother likes to use to describe me, because she likes people to leave me alone and let me fly around. When I was little, I used to watch bubbles form on the nose of my turtles for hours. In the country a lot like that is happening.

I think it would be nice for old people to work if earning money would be no problem. Like my grandmother works for the UN, and she wouldn't do that if she had to earn money. There are a lot of volunteer things, a lot of courses.

I'm in Project SCOPE II. They send teen workers into the women's homes. We talk to them, shop for them, tidy up, do odds and ends. All the women we visit are pretty stuck in their houses. They're tired and sickly, and they don't want to go outside. It's really a great program. A lot of people are paid, but there are also volunteers from the private schools. That's what I am. I see the same person every week. Miss Katherine Carlin. She lives in a building which, in other circumstances, I don't think I'd ever see. The building shouldn't be there. But she's lucky because she can pay low rent. They have no bells. I have a key, but when I forget my key, I open the door by pushing a piece of cardboard between the door. Everything's broken. It's a walk-up, and she lives on the fifth floor, and she's partially crippled.

I love to work with people, particularly old people. They've been around so long and have had so many experiences, and they know so much. You can really learn a lot from them. Basic emotions don't change. The same sadness or happiness has been around since the beginning of life. Miss Carlin's been through a lot, and I could listen to her talk for hours. She has a calling service, and if it wasn't there, she wouldn't even know if it was Monday or Tuesday. She's switched her entire day around, her entire week around. Why, she gets up at 2:00 A.M. for breakfast.

Miss Carlin has a very bad ankle, and she has pains in it. She's only seventy. But she's had a very hard, long working life. She is a miss; she never married. She's older than she should be. I have a grandmother who's seventy-four, and she's so sprightly you can't believe that she's older than this woman. And another grandmother who is one hundred and is still in good condition. She's funny, too, and has a really good sense of humor. I know Miss Carlin's history, and I know she's worked and was dependent on her money to eat. She hasn't saved very much. She has about $80 in the bank, and that's it. I don't think she's ever had a lot of money, so it doesn't frighten her to have so little. I've always had money, so the idea of my not having it would be very scary.

▽   L U C Y   M E R R I L L ,   A G E   15

I've had a very, very pleasant life. Even when we were poor, I enjoyed myself. Because I loved my sisters and brother. And I played the piano and I had a lot of friends and I had so many pupils who loved me. I never went into a home where I wasn't kissed and hugged before I started to teach. I was happy because everyone liked me.

I would live with anybody who loved me. But I wouldn't live with my daughter if she isn't willing to have me. I'd have to be an idiot. So I suffer here by myself. All the people that I knew who had to go to homes didn't live very long. I'm a very lucky woman for that reason. My income is less than $5000, and I live on that comfortably. I don't spend money on clothes, but I eat well. But I don't fix my home up any more.

▽   LILLIAN KROMICK, AGE 86

It's just like a small town here in our mobile park, and everybody is so thoughtful. You can't get acquainted in Leisure World like you do here. We feel we're in a little home of our own. Leisure World's bigger and more expensive than our mobile park. We're busy all the time. We have our "potluck" and our geographic travelogues, bridge, canasta, bowling, and square dancing. I still pay taxes: taxes to the man who owns this property. That's part of my rent. I also pay $200 taxes to the Motor Vehicle Bureau. The vehicle is called a mobile, not a trailer, and it's fifty-two feet long. It's what you can live in; though you couldn't take it out on the highway or go camping. There are wheels under this so it could be moved, after it's unhooked and unbolted. We've been here three years, and there's nobody I don't like.

▽   GEORGE KEYES, AGE 78

I'd like to live in a house and have a lot of people visit me, back and forth. If I had children, I'd want them to come and bring the grandchildren, if I had any. I would want them to take me out, not like somebody old who they'd have to watch what they said in front of —I'd want them to come right out and say exactly what they want.

KIM CAUGHMAN, AGE 15

Since most of the people who are old don't live with their families, they are alone. It would be better if they could live together and have some kind of contact; you know, maybe visit with other elderly people. Instead of seeing the same four walls every day, they'd see people. People they can relate to. I kind of picture them living in a big country place, coming and going as they please, without having to be in bed at a certain time. Just a bunch of them all living together. There's a project for older people on 70th Street, and when I went past, I noticed two or three of them standing outside chatting. And they looked nice. Now my grandparents don't talk to each other much. But on Saturdays my grandfather goes by himself to the race track. My grandmother just sits home. I hope when I'm their age, I'll be treated better than most old people are treated today.

JANETTE BECK, AGE 21

I don't want to think about illness. But that's another reason I feel so safe here at Leisure World, with the new hospital and the medical facilities. All I have to do is pick up my phone and have a doctor or a nurse here immediately. Where I came from in Arcadia, California, I didn't have that kind of help. Doctors just stopped coming to our home.

My husband and I decided before he passed away that some day we were going to live here. He always said if anything happened to him that I should go to Leisure World. Then I know, he said, that you'll be safe. I had to stay in our house, it was very large on several acres, while I settled the estate. We always liked the atmosphere here and the security. In my situation now, that is quite important to me. People are very friendly. You don't seem to be a stranger to anybody. They greet you with a warm smile. There's so many different kinds of recreation and crafts a person can get into. And they have many trips and tours. But whatever I do, I can come home and have no fear coming through that front gate and into this house.

I would love to travel and I have never been able to. We planned after my husband retired to do a lot of traveling. He was supposed to retire in 1956. I kept on asking him, "What year now?" He had five major heart attacks before he finally passed away. So we never did go. The one place he wanted to go visit was Sweden to see his relatives. He said to me, "Honey, I wish I had listened to you. I should have taken the time off and gone. Now look." So now I would like to travel. I'll go with people from Leisure World. I won't enjoy it as much as I would have if we had gone together. But I'm going with the thought that I will enjoy it and I'm going to meet people. I may even meet some other nice gentlemen.

JUNETH JOHNSON, AGE 66

LONELINESS

I've never been lonely in my life because I have so much to do. My wife is lonely. She likes people and needs activity around her. She's on the phone night and day to get some company. A lot of her friends are all dead. The fact is we have outlived the people we loved. The only loneliness I feel is for the people that are gone. How many people are there in this world that you can honestly say you miss because you loved them? I'm sorry that I didn't appreciate the people I loved when they were alive. I didn't do enough for them and they didn't do enough for me. I guess because I never gave them the chance. Anyway, we had no more than five or six good friends in our lifetime.

DR. LOUIS KUSHNER, AGE 87

I was extremely lonely when I first came to live here and faced retirement. It took me a long time to readjust to living on my own. Loneliness was a thing I had to deal with myself. I had to find people to get to know in this area which is notably snobby. But I do have plenty of resources and the kind of education and life that gives me many things to enjoy. Normally, I had found my friends in the church, but that's difficult here. It wasn't a very congenial church. As in most things, my family helped. My sons took me to the theaters and concerts and made the loneliness quite manageable. I think if I hadn't my resources and good family, I could easily turn inward and become bigoted.

F.M.BOWERS, AGE 73

I don't really feel lonely; it's only I fear being alone. I'm afraid that I might get up some day and find nobody around that I know. The people that live in this building move out too fast, and my other friends are too far away.

JOHN HOWARD, AGE 69

I'm never lonely. I can't understand why people get lonely. My idea of a good time is having a little time to myself. I have—and had—a full life. I had a son and a lot of looking-after-things to do. I speak all over the place at universities and schools. The universities love to have me come. It sort of encourages the kids who are worried about what's going to happen to them in later years. The teachers feel it's good exposing them to an older woman who isn't afraid of being an older woman.

HOPE BAGGER, AGE 84

MARRIAGE

I had many beaux, many proposals, but I thought of my family. I couldn't leave them. I had to help support them and, not only that, I was a big help to my mother. We lived in a private house with eight children, and there was lots to be done. I loved housework. Every morning I practiced the piano and my singing, and afterwards, before going to school, I had to take care of the little ones, diaper them, and make breakfast. I gave piano lessons when I was about fifteen, sixteen, and seventeen. I had about forty pupils and the fee gradually increased from fifty cents to two dollars a lesson. I didn't care very much about getting married. Maybe that's why I got married at thirty-two. I was an old maid.

LILLIAN KROMICK, AGE 86

My mother said, "Son, someday you may get married. And you might not stay with this woman . . . your wife. You must learn how to do something for yourself." She taught me to cook, to clean, and I told my wife when we got married, "Now listen, I know how to do some things for myself, and if you die before I do, or if you leave me, I can take care of myself." I got married because I thought it was time for me to get married.

ROSEL COHEN, AGE 68

I was studying music and singing all the time before I married. I was going to do operatic work; in fact, I had an audition with the Sol Hurok of our day. I don't know if you remember Madame Mazaran, who created the part of Elektra at the Manhattan Opera House. I knew someone who knew her, and she wanted me to audition. At that time I became engaged. I auditioned and she wanted me to give up everything, go to Paris with her and devote my entire life to music. But my future husband had different ideas. And he said, "I don't care what you do, but you'll never earn money for me. I'm going to be the breadwinner and you're not going to work. You can sing to your heart's content." He loved my singing. He said that I could go on with my singing and doing charitable work. My parents agreed with him. If they hadn't, I would have gone on. In those days we didn't say, "To hell with everybody else. I'll do as I please." My father agreed he was right for me. He was a very fine, upstanding man—an ambitious man—and I would probably have a very sweet life with him. That's all a girl needed in those days.

If it were today, I'm sure I would have gone to Paris. I was very upset because I did want to go. Music was my life in those days. It was all I cared about. And I gave it up. My parents said, "You may never get a chance to meet a man like that, and you may go out in the world and only meet tramps." I was about eighteen years old.

SUSAN ROBINSON, AGE 88

I was born in Austria. My parents were well off, and in the course of growing up, I had eleven proposals of marriage. My parents were well off, as I said, so that was the reason for most of the proposals. Besides, I was choosy. I went to Berlin, Germany, to study singing with a famous singer. It was my landlady who introduced me to the man who became my husband. He was a psychiatrist working in a mental institution. I was twenty-four and he was thirty-four, and he was the most wonderful man. My first thought in meeting him was that he could be "it." We discovered that we had all the same interests, particularly tennis and chess.

MIMI MARTIN, AGE 88

We Germans are different. We know we can't live on love, so we have to get established before we marry. We have to have a little bit of money. You save your pennies, your dollars, and *then* you get married. You have to have at least a three-room apartment. That's the rule. And the husband should have a good job. A steady job.

We were very respectable, my husband and I. We lived in New Jersey. We both worked very hard. We had a five-room bungalow, which we enjoyed very much. And we said when we reached sixty-five, we both would retire or give up. Then we were going to enjoy life. In a way, we got our wishes. We were ambitious people

and lived very respectably. If you want something, you work for it; else you haven't got anything. By respectable, I mean we never had somebody knocking on our door asking for payment for something we bought. We never bought till we had the money. Some people have debts all over. Not us.

I didn't know before I married that I loved him in a certain respect. You know teen-agers picture love entirely differently. Marriage means only romance. It's all right if you're in love, but don't go overboard, I say to them. . . . They should meet a lot of people. Each one has a different idea and character and some have ways you like. You never find a perfect mate. If you think so, you're so in love that you can't see. Romance doesn't keep up the way it is at the beginning. But the longer you live together, the more important you are for each other. You get used to each other in so many different ways.

LEOPOLDINA KRAUSE, AGE 73

I never wanted to marry, but time was running out, so I thought I'd better grab this one. I didn't love him when I married . . . I learned to as we got older. He didn't have much in the way of security, but I was getting older. All my friends that I grew up with were married. Even my mother said, "Marry him." So I said yes. I felt it was time to get married. I was about twenty-eight. I'd been having a good time in life—you know what I mean. I found I still had a good time after I married. We went out together, we'd drink together, play cards together, we smoked together. Whatever he'd do, I'd do.

ROXIE COHEN, AGE 67

MOMENTS

The beautiful moments of my life have been with my children. I say, "Thank God, they are on their own." They want no help from Papa. Not that they would get it. They never really asked for it. My daughter's children are great and will be great. To me, that means accomplishment. What you leave behind in life is what counts; then you're part of the future. You may not be here to enjoy it, but the future is what you've worked for.

DR. LOUIS KUSHNER, AGE 87

My best moments happened during my marriage. We fitted together like a watch. He was absolutely marvelous. Once he said that I was the most intelligent woman he ever met. His death was hard for me, but I'm glad he died when he did. The Nazis would have treated him terribly. They were unbelievable, absolutely inhuman. It was my children that kept me going.

MIMI MARTIN, AGE 88 ▷

My wife's happiest moments were when she truly met me. And when I met her. Seriously, I think that was a very happy moment in my life.

▽   ROSEL COHEN, AGE 68

MONEY

I'm living on borrowed time at my age. When you've retired, you are living on borrowed time, aren't you? I'm not worried, provided inflation doesn't go mad. If I couldn't afford to have a telephone, and I had to sell my personal possessions and clothes, I'd hate to live having only one suit of clothes and one shirt. New ones could be obtained from the Social Services (of our City Government). There again, you have to be almost broke. Age Concern—my old-age group—runs an employment agency. But they offer only menial jobs, and a man or woman isn't paid what he's worth. The State permits you only to earn, say, about $30 a week. If you earn more, they reduce your pension, and I barely manage on mine. That's wrong.

FRED WOOLEY, AGE 68

People where I live respect the fact that I have a little more than they have. Maybe because I live in a better home than they do. People respect money and wealth to a greater degree than they respect knowledge. It's how much you've got in the bank and how much you socialize that counts. That's what I found out in life.

DR. LOUIS KUSHNER, AGE 87

The secret of living is that you live up to every minute with what you can afford. We never lived beyond our means. My wife always took a portion of the money I made and put it aside. I'd invest it and the money multiplied. She is a saver, and I owe the money I have now to her.

DR. LOUIS KUSHNER, AGE 87

NURSING HOMES

It's a terrible thing and a great fear of many of the older people: to go to a nursing home. That's why senior citizen homes are springing up. The children will say, "Go into a home and we'll still do the best we can. But we can't keep you at home or in an apartment. We have enough troubles of our own." They have their families, their wives. Wives play a big part in the way a son will treat his mother.

SUSAN ROBINSON, AGE 88

I used to have two good old friends at the nursing home here last summer. Their names were Mr. and Mrs. Steifel, I think. He lived in one wing of the home and she in the other. They were always separated. She was sick a lot and he used to fall a lot. That's why they had to tie him to his wheelchair because he always wanted to try to walk. Lots of times he'd fall and I had to pick him up by myself. He always wanted to be near his wife. Sometimes I used to take him down in his wheelchair to the garden. He didn't like to talk, except to his wife. He always used to pat her hand and say, "I love you, I love you." And then he'd kiss her.

WILLIE LAZADO, AGE 15

I have a great-great-aunt, and she's really sick, and she lives in a nursing home. She hardly ever gets out of bed. It's so sad when you go to see her. She's so depressed. You know—she likes people to come and talk to her. She gets very lonely. Half the people there are all crunched up in their beds. It's really gross.

EMILY
Classroom interview

The whole unwanted thing of throwing old people into nursing homes—I'm not afraid of that, because it's just not part of the black society. We don't put old people into nursing homes; we just don't get rid of them. I'm not afraid of not having some place or somebody at all times. I think it's more the American White Culture. There are some blacks in nursing homes, but we just usually don't have the money to put anybody in a home. My grandfather lives with us now that his wife died. And we *love* it! He's always arguing, he's always making trouble—he's just become part of our daily lives. My grandfather in a nursing home? I could never see it; it just wouldn't make any sense. He gets up every morning at six-thirty and he goes to work. He fixes breakfast for us. He would never just sit around. I love him.

DAYNA BOWEN, AGE 15

Our society doesn't take care of old people. They do in Denmark, maybe because it's an open country. I used to live in a neighborhood where there were six nursing homes on one street. It was so depressing to walk by and see the old people sitting on the little stoops, doing nothing. I think nursing homes should be in the country, where people can roam around, say on about ten acres. It would be better than being in the city. And possibly they should be given work to do. I mean work in terms of the nursing home—secretarial work, filing in the office, caretaking, or even mowing the grass. Our government should take more responsibility.

ANTHONY SHANKS, AGE 16

POLITICAL AND SOCIAL ACTION

We at the Gray Panthers are working now on trying to get lists of doctors who will pay some attention to older patients. Usually, if you call a doctor in the middle of the night, he suggests aspirin, and if you're still alive the next morning, to come to his office. One reason is they can't make enough money on us older people, and the kind of sicknesses that happen to us are not interesting to most doctors: arthritis, hypertension, for example. In addition, most of them have no geriatric training. There are only two medical schools in this very large city of New York that pay any attention to old people.

The Teachers College of Columbia University cooperated with Ralph Nader, and the Gray Panthers volunteered to investigate whether dealers were selling unneeded hearing aids. Sure enough, they were. I personally visited fifteen dealers, and every last one tried to sell me a hearing aid. Teachers College had tested me and discovered that no hearing aid could improve my hearing. All our findings were sent to Albany and stopped a bill from passing, which wouldn't have been helpful to anyone with a hearing problem.

When I was seventy, after traveling alone and having a good time, I got myself a job. My job was finding jobs for people, and that's how I found out how hard it is for older people to get work. So I decided then and there that I was working from seventy to eighty, but when I got to be eighty, I had to retire. The first thing I did at eighty was to contact the United States Senate Committee on Aging. I wrote them what I thought about their "Retirement at sixty-five" law. We had a lot of correspondence, but I began to work closer to home on the New York State Legislature. Two bills changing this law are sitting in the Assembly and Senate now that haven't yet passed.

Next year I plan to do more work.

▽ HOPE BAGGER, AGE 84

RELATIONSHIPS

My wife's been beautiful. She's a beautiful woman. I've never heard her say a nasty thing to anybody. She's much better than I am. I don't deserve her. That's the truth. Being with her is enough compensation for me. I think God is good to me because of her. If there's any woman who's going to enter the Kingdom of Heaven, she will and sit in the front row.

DR. LOUIS KUSHNER, AGE 87

I remember urging a group of students attending an Institute for Social Progress get-together—who were congregating by color—to associate with other people, not with people having similar problems to theirs. Get out and find out, I said. That was always the best way for me.

The State should support a program teaching

the elderly how to improve their condition. The program should include younger people who will someday be old. I don't think any senior center should be open unless it requires that people have discussions on social issues. One day I was talking to a senior group about health delivery services and how one health plan is better than another. The group said it was the Government's responsibility. "That's not what we're discussing now," I said. "If you'd like to stay later, we'll discuss Government." And they stayed later after class, three more hours. Courses in those "College at sixty" programs should teach Knowledge of Government and How to Find Your Way in a Bureaucracy, and especially courses that demonstrate how to engage in social-action programs for everyone's benefit.

HOPE BAGGER, AGE 84

I was asked to go to a meeting of an Action Group, and I got involved. We do need friendships with people our own age. Most clubs stress doing things that are *good* for you. We've got "to amuse you," they say, so "you'll do Bingo" or "you'll do basket work."

Why should I do basket work? I've never done it. And I don't want to. And I hate Bingo.

◁ FRED WOOLEY, AGE 68

REMARRIAGE

It's very often I think to myself, "If only someone were here with me now." Otherwise I don't want it. I'm glad to be alone. I've lived alone for twenty years. I know there are a lot of marriages at my age. You know what? I give them credit. It does give you companionship to see another human being, even if he's in the next room. It is a wonderful thing, if you can stand each other at our age. We gave a ride to a lady going home from a wedding recently. She said she was going to Mount Sinai Hospital. That's where her second husband was. Two years ago she had married him after her husband died. She said bitterly, "I was getting along fine and I had to get married again. Now I live at the hospital." I just had one husband, and that was the end of it for me. I never cared too much for men anyhow. Except for my husband. That was sacred.

No one else tempted me. I've never gone to a place yet where I didn't have a man come over and ask me if I wouldn't go out with him. If I went, it would make me feel very bad. That's that old saying, "You can't teach an old dog new tricks." I've gotten old by myself, and I know just what I want to do and how I want to do it. . . . I couldn't take on anybody else's eccentricities.

SUSAN ROBINSON, AGE 88

There are about six or eight older fellows in this block where I live, and each and every one of them is either single, divorced, or widowed. And I don't see any mad rush to remarry. In England it's more companionship than sex that interests us if we do remarry. After you're sixty-seven, a pretty girl just doesn't get you worked up.

FRED WOOLEY, AGE 68

I have no thoughts of remarriage now. I want to be independent, live my own life, and maybe the day will come when I find somebody. Perhaps a nice gentleman whose companionship I would enjoy. We could go to the theater, the opera, the ballet, or to dinner. That would be fine.

▽ JUNETH JOHNSON, AGE 66

RETIREMENT

I don't feel old at all. I can't stay in bed after 8:00 A.M. I get up in the morning and I do my exercise and I take my long walk daily. When I go to bed at night, I'm loosened up. I feel good. I've been off the job exactly two years. I'm living on my Social Security. I don't worry about the future. I figure I worked thirty-four years and it was long enough. I could continue work, but I said when I got to be sixty-five, I'd retire.

ROSEL COHEN, AGE 68

I don't think we treat old people fairly—the whole thing, retiring them at sixty-five, thinking they're useless, not giving them work, inadequate insurance. After sixty-five, forget it! You can't get a loan because you're going to die tomorrow, so, "We can't trust our money with you." People are so afraid of going over the hill— finished after thirty.

The only thing I can think of is for people to look at others as individuals. Because there are some people who can't work after twenty! And there are others who can work until they're ninety-seven. My Grandfather Cohen loves retirement. He could have retired when he was thirty. My other grandfather won't. If he were working in an institution, he would have had to stop work. And that would have made him miserable. It's just lucky that he was in business for himself and continues working. It's his business that keeps him going. He's about seventy-one, I think. At sixty-five, that's the end of everything. Why not the beginning? When I retire, it's going to be a happy day. I won't have to work any more. When I get ready —I'm ready to retire now.

DAYNA BOWEN, AGE 15 ▷

When I began to work, I looked forward to retirement. You know, you say to yourself, "Thank God, I can retire." I was always thinking that much ahead. Even when I was twenty.

Our trade union had a subscription scheme. You paid in for your pension, granted on retirement. I've been retired now two years, a year earlier than I should have because I had heart trouble. Now, you don't get a magnificent retirement sum, just a few dollars a week. When I worked, I was a printer's reader, which means I read and corrected newspaper proof.

Time passes now just as quickly as it has at any other time. I got up at about seven this morning, and before I knew it, it was nine. I was just trying to do the paper's crossword puzzle, which I wouldn't have time to do if I was working.

When you retire, you always hope that you'll get about, travel and see people. I used to go to Somerset to see a friend of mine, but he's dead. As the friends drop out, you have less and less to see. Your world diminishes.

FRED WOOLEY, AGE 68

SEX

I used to get a guide from the Lighthouse to take me to the doctor; I can't go alone. The guide had glaucoma, and his sight got so bad he, too, finally couldn't go out any more. No, I wouldn't invite that man up here, because he's a widower and people might talk. And I care about my reputation. All those men only wanted sex and I didn't—even the older men. The eighty-year-olds—no. They don't even go out any more. But that's all the others are out for. I wouldn't do it. Why should I be somebody else's handkerchief? I heard gossip in the Senior Citizens Club about other women when I used to go. "She is a regular tart," they'd say. Not me!

LEOPOLDINA KRAUSE, AGE 73

Everybody's talking about how depressing it's going to be to get old. I mean—why can't they have *something* to make them happy?!

MARC
Classroom interview

I can't imagine old people having sex.
Classroom interview
(tape recording unclear, name unknown)

If it's possible with young people, it's possible with old people. I feel if it's gotta be done, it's gotta be done. They have as much right to pleasure as young people do.

DAVID WALKER, AGE 14

It's weird. Old people shouldn't have sex. It's not right when a lady has sex. It's OK for men. Ladies may get pregnant. If they're married, it's up to them. Even so, it bothers me anyway. And come to think of it, I don't think it's right for an old man, either.

▽ WILLIE LAZADO, AGE 15

I think that when people don't have sex when they're older, it's because of something when they're younger. For me, I can never imagine age hampering my sex life, or anything hampering my sex life.

LUCY MERRILL, AGE 15

Some people come around. I used to go to church and some of the members come and see me once in a while or call me on the phone. But when it comes to men (I'm still single), I don't bother with any of them. I don't want them pinching me and trying to get all they want . . . you know what I mean?

LENA ANDERSON, AGE 75

That's a joke. I discuss it with my grandmother all the time. When I go out and I know they're going to be alone, I sprinkle a little perfume on her, and I tell her, "Go ahead. Go find Papa." And she says, "Oh, Janette. That was done with forty years ago." She doesn't sleep with him at all. She sleeps in the same bed with me. They haven't for years. I think he's interested, but she's not.

▽ JANETTE BECK, AGE 21

I think they have a right to have sex whenever they want. But I can't imagine my mother and father having sex. It disgusts me. It doesn't feel right to me. It doesn't fit.

AARON
Classroom interview

I think it's fine if they can do it. They're people, too. It's part of life. It's not like they're alien to us. Everyone's going to be that way. I'm going to be that way.

ANTHONY SHANKS, AGE 16

It'd be pretty hard. What happens if one of them dies while they're doing it? Hunhh? *Oh, my God!* If they can do it and like it, why not? It's a free, open society. But I don't think they should have babies 'cause the two may die. The baby would then have no father and mother. But I think they might as well get as much fun as possible. It doesn't matter whether they're thirty or eighty.

▽ JOHN SHANKS, AGE 14

WHAT IS OLD?

When you feel like having somebody around, like your grandchildren and children.

JAN
Classroom interview

It's deeply frustrating to be old. You can't do things you want to. So you want to, but you can't. And you have to see a doctor much more.

AARON
Classroom interview

I think it's in your mind.

ANDRE
Classroom interview

Sixty is old. I mean, not *old* old. But that's beginning to get old.

LUCY MERRILL, AGE 15

My grandmother is only fifty-nine, and she acts very old. She goes to work, but she's always sick. She always coughs. She's never all right. When she comes to our house, she never laughs. So I think when you're sick, you're old.

ANGELA
Classroom interview

It's like being more of a *nothing* than a something. When I was six, I thought twenty was like, "Oh, my God, that's old!" And now ninety is terribly old. Still, when I think of someone who's forty . . . It's what's old to you.

If you're not dependent on somebody, you're not old.

MARK
Classroom interview

You're old when your mind gives out, when you can't think straight, and you can't change.

KATHY
Classroom interview

Some people might feel it's nice being old, because after all your frivolous years, you finally have a rest.

DAVID
Classroom interview

WIDOWHOOD

My best moments were mostly family joys, my marriage and falling in love. I think love becomes joy, deeper than mere pleasure, when you find it's not a flash in the pan but a lasting relationship. I took a great risk when I married a man a great deal older than myself. I took a long time to decide, and to wrench myself away from teaching. But my main continuing joy has come from my relationship with my husband. He died after thirteen years of marriage. That was my lowest point. I had to go back to work, because I had to face my financial situation for the first time alone, and I had two children to educate. It was a question of their future, and you really had to press on. And you do. The boys and I tried to make decisions together. They were eleven and twelve years old at the time. It was healthier for us to share our difficulties. It seems to have proved to be the right thing to do.

F. M. BOWERS, AGE 73

I was married to Mr. Robinson about forty-four or forty-six years. He's gone twenty years the twentieth of October. I've been alone twenty years. It's an entirely different world and a big shock when a man dies. It's such an awakening, because the people you thought were your very good friends were the first to get away. They're afraid you might be on their hands. They tell you, "Now, don't forget, call me when you need me." And when I did need them, I never saw them. You never get adjusted to being a widow. Never. I'm very, very lonesome. Sometimes I'm alone here at night and without realizing it, the tears come to my eyes and I say, "Now, Susie, what are you crying about now?" I talk to myself. I should have a silly dog and let him bark at me.

SUSAN ROBINSON, AGE 88

I was told never to use that word "widow" at Leisure World. I asked them why. They said, "As far as we're concerned, you're a single woman." I said, "That still doesn't answer my question. Why should I not refer to myself as a widow?" They said, "It's too depressing. That life is behind you, and now you must lead a new life, have a new adventure." But I must admit, when I moved here and unpacked all my belongings, it was very lonesome.

JUNETH JOHNSON, AGE 66

Widowhood is terrible. You live a life with a man or woman for sixty years and when that man or woman goes, the calamity is incomparable.

DR. LOUIS KUSHNER, AGE 87

WORK

I started out taking piano lessons because at thirteen my voice was so beautiful that I used to be pulled out from assembly to lead my school. I'd stand on the platform and sing. My voice was very mature. It wasn't like a young child's voice at all. My "career" started when McKinley died. He was assassinated when he was President. Everybody in all the schools was singing "Nearer My God to Thee." They asked me to sing it on the platform. I did and everybody cried. When I came home and sang it for my father, he cried, too. We had company for supper on Sunday night. My father said, "You should hear Lily sing 'Nearer My God to Thee.' She's shy, so she'll sing it in the kitchen for you when she does the dishes." I did. All the guests jumped down my father's throat and said, "Get a piano. Get a piano quickly. That child has a marvelous voice." The next day my father went to Wanamaker's department store and bought my first piano for $175.

LILLIAN KROMICK, AGE 86

THE YOUNG TALK

ABOUT THE OLD

The person I work for in Project SCOPE—I've seen pictures of her when she was younger. She was beautiful. She was *so* beautiful. And she used to do modeling when she was young. She has a gorgeous painting of her in her house, and I've also seen photographs of her (she did naked modeling, too, for art things), and I've seen her naked now. And she was so beautiful. At first it kind of scared me. Because I saw both at the same time. I figured out, by the two pictures of her, how I'd look when I'm old. She's not ugly, she's just—old. Wrinkled and kind of beautiful.

Miss Carlin (that's her name) is a hoarder. She lives in a very small apartment covered with junk. Every week it's a long, long process for her to clear a seat for me to sit down in. One time I was putting a light bulb in, and we had to open a ladder. It took nearly an hour to clear a space for that ladder. At first it scared me to walk in there. After a while it got homey. I was uncomfortable when I first went there. It's crazy. There are cockroaches crawling everywhere, newspapers piled high. Every time you move, something falls over. And without an elevator man like I'm used to, the place isn't so safe. Her whole existence is a little shabby. She usually is in her bathrobe. One of them has buttons, and they're always undone. I'm always reaching over and saying, "Naughty, naughty." We really

get along well. I'm not uncomfortable with her any more.

She's like a taste, in a way. She's all kind of all mellow and old . . . like good times and bad times all woven together. She's like an oasis in a week of trauma. When I have a week of vacation, I usually get into a sleep pattern equal to hers. We're a lot alike. We're kind of misty. Although being with her takes a bit of control, and a lot of work—like running around to fifty stores to find an item no one else carries. But she loves me. And I love her.

LUCY MERRILL, AGE 15

When I've been sick I felt like an old man. You're in bed and you feel so blah. You feel left out and you feel sad. Then you have nothing to do. And you sleep and sleep. Nobody's there to talk to. If someone would be there, it'd be nice.

I guess you always picture people in the street and you go, "Oh, my God, that may look like me." That guy is about to turn into a peach. Or he looks like a raisin.

You don't want to look crouched over, have a limp and no teeth! You know, like the all-American old man.

JOHN SHANKS, AGE 14

I guess it's their character, but I like to talk to old people. They've been where I am now, and I feel they can give me some hints about what's going to happen to me. One client talks to me about my education. She wants me to stay in school, then latch on to a better job and keep going higher. I may want to be a legal secretary.

KIM CAUGHMAN, AGE 15

Some old people I work with I don't get along with. But some of them I'd go visit whether I worked for them or not. It's the way some of them live, rats and cockroaches, so I didn't want to stay with them. I just wanted to get out. I've found that the ones who trust me are the ones I sit and talk to after my errands for them are done. Some ask, "How was school today? How's your boyfriend?" Those are the ones I can sit and talk to. I have Mrs. Shaw I'm very close to. Then I had Miss Osser who I used to hate going to. We used to fight constantly. We really used to yell at each other. One day I went there and she looked so far away. I said, "What's the matter?" She told me she was

eighty-eight years old and she thinks she's going senile. She knew she was. She was right. And she's so afraid, she said. I started talking with her, and we got to be pretty close. I finally sat and listened to her for once. Now I like her a lot.

The old people I take care of through the Lenox Hill Neighborhood Association make a big deal out of my coming to see them. They get ready for days ahead. And if I don't come or if I'm late, they call up Lenox Hill, then my house—not to get me in trouble, but to say, "Where's Janette? Is she sick? Has something happened?" When I first took the job, I was just doing it for the money—$2.25 an hour. I thought, "Oh, this is great—you have so much freedom with this job. Nobody knows if I'm coming. . . ." And then you see how these people wait for you, and you begin to feel responsible for them. And you have to see them, because you're the only one who cares. Many have told me, if it weren't for me, they didn't know what they would do.

JANETTE BECK, AGE 21

You may grow gray and white on the outside, but inside you can still be the same person you were thirty years ago. It upsets me to think of someone being a vegetable. If you can't move, life is not worth living. It wouldn't be much fun not being able to do anything, even if you have a thousand maids and servants. But I couldn't kill myself. I couldn't go through with that.

Being old does increase your wisdom. And you can take it easier, because you don't rush into things as fast.

◁ DAVID WALKER, AGE 14

A PORTFOLIO
OF PHOTOGRAPHS
OF THE AGED

BIBLIOGRAPHY

Butler, Robert N., M.D. *Why Survive? Being Old in America.*
New York: Harper & Row, 1975.
———, and Lewis, Myrna, A.C.S.W. *Aging and Mental Health.*
New York: C. V. Mosby & Co., 1973.
Cherry, Lawrence and Rona. "Slowing the Clock of Age." *The
New York Times Sunday Magazine,* May 12, 1974.
Curtin, Sharon R. *Nobody Ever Died of Old Age.* Boston:
Atlantic Monthly Press, 1973.
De Beauvoir, Simone. *The Coming of Age.* New York:
G. P. Putnam's Sons, 1972. Paperback edition: Paperback
Library, 1973.
———. "Frank Talk on a Forbidden Subject." *The New York
Times Sunday Magazine,* March 26, 1972.
Fritz, Dorothy B. *Growing Old Is a Family Affair.* Richmond,
Va.: John Knox Press, Paperback.
Harper's Magazine. "Report on Longevity: Ah, To Be Young
While Old," June 1973, pp. 3–10.
Hendin, David. *Death as a Fact of Life.* New York:
W. W. Norton & Co., 1973. Paperback edition: Warner
Paperback Library, 1974.
Jacoby, Susan. "Waiting for the End: On Nursing Homes." *The
New York Times Sunday Magazine,* March 31, 1974.
Johnson, Sheila K. *Idle Haven.* University of California Press,
1971.
Jury, Mark, and Jury, Dan. *Gramp.* New York: Grossman
Publishers, 1976.
Knopf, Olga, M.D. *Successful Aging.* New York: The Viking
Press, 1975.
Kubler-Ross, Elisabeth, M.D. *On Death and Dying.* New York:
The Macmillan Co., 1970.
L'Engle, Madeleine. *The Summer of the Great Grandmother.*
New York: Farrar, Straus & Giroux, 1974.
Liang, Daniel S. *Facts About Aging.* Springfield, Ill.:
C. C. Thomas Publications Paperback.
Lobsenz, Norman. "Sex and the Senior Citizen." *The New York
Times Sunday Magazine,* January 20, 1974.
Mead, Margaret. *Culture and Commitment.* New York:
Doubleday & Co., 1970.
Mendelson, Mary. *Tender Loving Greed.* New York: Alfred A.
Knopf, Inc., 1974.
Ms. Magazine. "When Is Old?—How to Beat Age Bias." June
1975.
Ms. "Gazette." "Pension, Welfare Reform and Social Security."
March 1975, pp. 97–100.

Nader, Ralph, and Blackwell, Kate. *You and Your Pension.* New
York: Grossman Publishers, 1973.
Note: A list of Nader books can be obtained from: Public
Citizen, P. O. Box 14404, Washington, D.C. 20036.
The New York Times. "They're All Past Sixty . . . Retired and
All Are Trying To Help." May 17, 1974, p. 34.
Newsweek Magazine. "Can Aging Be Cured?" April 16, 1973.
Pearce, Donn. *Dying in the Sun.* New York: Charter House
(Division of David McKay Co.), 1974.
People Magazine. "Gray Panther, Maggie Kuhn." October 26,
1975, pp. 29–32.
Rogers, Carl R. *On Becoming a Person.* Boston: Houghton
Mifflin Company (Sentry Edition), 1961.
Stern, Edith, and Ross, Mabel. *You and Your Aging Parents.*
New York: Harper & Row, 1965.
Tardiff, Olive. *How to Live Happily with Your Retired Husband.*
New York: Pilot Books, 1973. Paperback.
Time Magazine. "The Old in the Country of the Young."
August 3, 1970.
Time Magazine. "Old Age: How to Help our Parents." June 2,
1975, pp. 44–51.
"Toward a Public Policy on Mental Health Care of the Elderly"
—Formulated by the Committee on Aging of the Group for
the Advancement of Psychiatry, 1970. Park Avenue at 50th
St., New York, N.Y. 10016.
Townsend, Claire (Project Director). *Old Age, the Last
Segregation: The Report on Nursing Homes* (Ralph Nader's
Study Group Reports). New York: Grossman Publishers, 1971.
Unitarian Church. "Developing an Extended Family Program"
(pamphlet). 1535 Santa Barbara St., Santa Barbara, Cal.
White House Conference on Aging: "Toward a National Policy
on Aging." 2 volumes, U.S. Government Printing Office,
Washington, D.C. 20402, 1971–1973.
(Education; Employment; Facilities, Programs and Services;
Government and Non-Government Organizations; Physical
and Mental Health; Housing the Elderly; Nutrition; Planning;
Retirement; Retirement Roles and Activities; Research and
Demonstration; Spiritual Well-Being; Training; Transporta-
tion.)
Wolf, Anna W. M. *Helping Your Child to Understand Death.*
New York, N.Y. Child Study Press, 1973.

PUBLIC AFFAIRS PAMPHLETS—381 Park Avenue South,
New York, N.Y. 10016. 35¢ each.

#501—After 65—Resources for Self-Reliance, Theodore Irwin
#327—A Full Life After 65, Edith M. Stern
#446—Better Health in Later Years
#336—Food Hints for Mature People
#182-A—Getting Ready to Retire, Katherine Close
#519—Sex After 65, Norman Lobsenz
National Council on Aging, 1828 "L" Street N.W.,
Washington, D.C. 20036—such subjects as: Housing,
Retirement, Nutrition, Legal Problems, Employment, Minority
Groups, Bibliographies.

MAGAZINES

AARP: Modern Maturity, 215 Long Beach Blvd., Long Beach,
Cal. 90801. $2.00 per year.

Retirement Living, 150 E. 58th St., New York, N.Y. 10022. $6.75
per year. (Plus special Guidebooks on Housing, Health,
Money, the Law, Leisure and Planning.)

Prime Time, 168 W. 86th St., Apt. 9A, New York, N.Y. 10024.
$7.00 per year. A newsletter for mature women.

New York Handbook: A Resource Guide for Older Yorkers,
1973. (*New York Magazine*, 196 E. 21st St., New York, N.Y.
10016) 25¢.

16 MM FILMS ON AGING

Harry and Tonto. 1974. Director: Paul Mazursky. Distributor:
Films, Inc., 733 Greenbay Road, Wilmette, Ill. 60091.

Koch. 1971. Director: Jack Lemmon. Distributor: Films, Inc.,
733 Greenbay Road, Wilmette, Ill. 60091.

Nell and Fred. 1971. Director: Richard Todd. Distributor:
McGraw-Hill Films, 1221 Avenue of the Americas, New York,
N.Y. 10020.

Old-Fashioned Woman. 1974. Director: Martha Coolidge. Distributor: Films, Inc., 733 Greenbay Road, Wilmette, Ill.
60091.

Peege. 1973. Director: Randal Kleiser. Distributor: Phoenix
Films, 470 Park Avenue South, New York, N.Y. 10016.

The Family of Man: Old Age. 1970. Producer: John Percival.
Distributor: Time-Life Films, 100 Eisenhower Drive, Paramus,
N.J. 07652.

When Parents Grow Old. 1973. Director: Gilbert Cates. Dis-
tributor: (fifteen-minute excerpt from the feature film *I Never
Sang For My Father*), Learning Corporation of America,
1350 Avenue of the Americas, New York, N.Y. 10019.
Distributor: (ninety-two-minute.) Macmillian Audio Brandon
Films, Inc., 34 MacQuesten Parkway South, Mount Vernon,
N.Y. 10550.

Note: Write the Educational Film Library Association, 17 West
60 Street, New York, N.Y. 10023, for their extensive
16mm-film catalogue or "filmography" by Judith Trojan on
aging.

ORGANIZATIONS

American Association of Retired Persons, 1909 "K" St.,
Washington, D.C. 20006. You receive *Modern Maturity*.
Annual dues: $2.00.

F.D.S., A Magazine of Young People's Liberation, of Ann Arbor,
Mich. 2007 Washenaw Ave., Ann Arbor, Mich. 48104
(affiliated with the Center for Research on Children and
Youth).

Gerontological Society, One DuPont Circle, Suite 250,
Washington, D.C. 20036. You receive two quarterly journals.
$25.00.

Gray Panthers, % Ethical Culture Society, 2 West 64th St., New
York, N.Y. 10023. Main Office: Gray Panthers, 3700 Chestnut
St., Philadelphia, Pa. 19104.

International Senior Citizens Association, 11753 Wilshire Blvd.,
Los Angeles, Cal. 90025 (you receive their published
newsletter).

O.W.L., The Older Woman's Lib, 434 E. 66th St., Oakland, Cal.
94609.

Task Force on Older Women, NOW, 28 E. 56th St., New York,
N.Y. 10022.